Dear Debt

A Story About
Breaking Up With Debt

Melanie Lockert

ISBN: 0692684808
ISBN-13: 978-0692684801

To my love and my family for always believing
in me, as well as the countless others fighting their
own journey out of debt.

TABLE OF CONTENTS

Part 4: Lessons from Paying Off Debt

INTRODUCTION

I bet you picked up this book to learn a little bit about the way money works, and how to get out of debt. Wild guess? You've come to the right place. In this book, we'll break down how to get out of debt, save money, earn more money, and live a life you love. Sounds great, right? But who am I, anyway? Why am I, of all people, writing a book about money? How is a theater major and former nonprofit employee qualified to talk about money? It's quite a funny story, really, which is what I hope to share with you throughout this book. Suffice it to say that I learned about money from the best teacher around: experience. Throughout my life, my choices have forced me to learn about money. Something I resisted so fiercely is now something I am fiercely passionate about.

I'm writing this book not only to tell my story of getting out of student loan debt, but to inspire a generation of young men and women saddled with debt to write their own stories of freedom. I paid off $81,000 in student loans without making six figures or living with my parents. Getting out of debt was the hardest thing I've ever done, but it has taught me so many lessons about life and money that I want to share with you. Debt does not have to be forever. You can ditch debt for its friends, Savings and Investing. Money doesn't have to be complicated, and more importantly it doesn't have to be inherently bad or reflect your self-worth.

This book is for anyone who has ever felt like they would never get out of debt. This book is for all student loan borrowers, or anyone who feels crushed under the weight of debt. If you feel like there has got to be a better way to manage your money, pay off debt, and forge your own path, this book is for you. I'm here to tell you that you are not alone. I'm here to tell you that getting out of debt is possible. It's not just a pipe dream. There is a better way to live, and I want to show you how. By sharing my journey, I hope to inspire you to pay off your debt, earn more money, and feel awesome about your financial choices and your life. In the end, you deserve to live a life that matters, not one that is weighed down by debt, interest payments, and debt collectors.

It's time to break up with debt.

Why is money important, anyway? Money: this one word can elicit a lot of emotions. It can bring out stress, anxiety, depression, greed, happiness, and joy in all of us. Many people often feel like there's never enough money. Or, if you are like I used to be, you think money represents power: the separation between the haves and the have-nots. I was placed squarely in the "have-nots" section. I would never be rich. I would never have a lot of money. I'd always have just enough to get by. As a creative person, I always thought money and art were two separate things. I thought that you had to struggle to survive, and that's the way things had to be. But after living on ten dollars to twelve dollars an hour and spending periods of time on food stamps, I have to say there's nothing cute or fun about being broke. People like to say that money isn't everything. While that's true to an extent, I firmly believe the only people who say that are people who haven't been face-to-face with being broke or feeling buried under debt.

Once upon a time, I was that person that didn't think money was important—that was until I didn't have much money left and was struggling to get by. Suddenly, my options felt so restricted. There were no choices on the table. The only choice was the free or cheapest option. When you have no money, your life choices are narrowed, which can leave you stagnant, stuck, or worse, in a depressing situation. Imagine that you're in a dead-end job and your boss is making your life miserable, but you can't quit because you can't afford to leave the job. Imagine that after living with your boyfriend or girlfriend, you realize that he or she isn't right for you, but you can't afford to live on your own, so you stay. Think of that childhood dream that you may have buried long ago. Did part of you bury it because it wasn't "practical"? What do all of these situations have in common? It's the difference between action and inaction. Having money means having choices. Once I realized this, I started to change my relationship with money.

I used to think that money was evil and that having money was only for the rich. However, it became clear to me that money is just a tool. Money is not inherently good or bad. It doesn't have a moral compass or a soul. We attribute our own feelings to it, but money itself is simply a tool for opportunities. Being able to have "walking-around money" or a "go to hell fund" can be a lifesaver. It can change the direction of your life and let you make the best choices for you based on what you think is best for you, rather than what you need financially.

Money is important because it puts a roof over your head. It puts food on the table. It gives you the choice to stay or go. It gives you opportunities. While I do believe some of the best things in life are free, such as your health, love, family, and friendships, oftentimes our goals and dreams come at a monetary cost. You should be able to unabashedly go after all your hopes and dreams, and let your money help you get there. No one is meant to just work, pay bills, put money toward debt, and repeat. Life is meant to be lived and enjoyed...and some things cost money.

The one thing that changed my life for the better was changing my relationship with money and how I thought about it. I stopped thinking that I was meant to be broke, or even deserved to be broke. I began to take action instead of dwelling on disappointments and complaining about all the things I couldn't do or things that I felt were out of my control. After transforming my relationship with money, something interesting started to change. I committed to paying off debt and paid off all $81,000 of my student loans. I started to earn more through side hustling. I launched a new career, writing about, of all things, money.

Having money in the bank has been a security blanket that has gotten me through tough times. Money also fueled me to quit my low-paying nonprofit job and become my own boss. Money has allowed me to travel to see friends and family at a moment's notice. It has allowed me to say "yes" more often than "no." If there's anything I want to teach you with this book, it's that money is not the enemy. Money is your friend—and if you work hard enough, it can be your best friend, and work hard for you in return.

Before reading on, I want you to think about:
- What is your relationship with money?
- How would making more money impact your life? How would making $100 more per month affect your life? $500? $1,000? Write it down.
- What is your dream salary? Think of the number, take out a check (if you have one of those soon-to-be relics), and make it out to yourself in the future, with your dream salary written on it. Keep your check on your desk.
- What negative money baggage are you carrying around? These include long-held assumptions about the way money works, or things your parents taught you about money that no longer serve you (e.g. money is evil, I'm a starving artist, etc.)

There are DIY worksheets at the end of this book to help you along your journey. Use them as you please.

PART 1

My Journey Into Debt

CHAPTER 1

The Moment That Changed Everything

Upon graduating from high school, I signed on the dotted line and took out student loans to attend college. Little did I know, debt and I would have a long-term affair that would last over a decade. At the time, I was seventeen years old and very naive. I had a vague idea of what student loans were—but really, I only knew they would help me attend college. Not going to college wasn't something I considered, so I simply accepted my student loans as part of the process, without knowing how they worked and the impact they'd have on my life going forward.

It wasn't until after I graduated from college that I understood the ramifications of taking out student loans. I graduated with a degree in theater and was wondering what to do with my life. After completing exit counseling on my federal student loans, I realized that I had amassed $23,000 in student loan debt. I thought that I had borrowed $18,000, but I failed to understand how interest actually worked. Some of my loans had been accruing interest during all four years of college. In that moment, student loans and interest started to finally make sense. I was disheartened by how much I owed and wondered how in the heck I was going to pay it back. I was twenty-two years old, without a full-time job, still living with my parents, and saddled with debt. I wasn't sure what to do.

Within six months' time, I did get a job—a low wage, nonprofit job in arts education, starting at $30,000 per year. I moved out of my parents' house and got my own studio apartment, but that salary didn't go very far in Los Angeles. I ended up treating my student loans like any other bill and simply paid the minimum balance each month, nothing more, nothing less. I figured that I had ten years to pay off my student loans, so I would worry about them later.

For the next several years, I enjoyed being a twenty-something living in LA. I frequented bars and restaurants and took advantage of the live music scene. Even as my salary increased to $38,000, I still only paid the minimum balance on my loans, which in hindsight, was a mistake. If you make more, you should put more toward debt! I made all the excuses in the book: I couldn't afford it, I didn't earn enough, I could pay off my loans "later." I was still so young and wanted to have fun, so I didn't prioritize my debt. After all, I thought student loans were considered the "good kind of debt." It wasn't until a business trip to New York that everything changed.

I was in New York City visiting New York University (NYU) for work. While I was there, I thought I'd simply check out their graduate school offerings. Getting a master's degree was something that I had always considered from afar, but never took too seriously up until that point. Once I was in New York, I fell in love with the city and NYU. When I flew back home, I decided, just for fun, to apply to New York University and another graduate school in Los Angeles. Getting a master's degree was on my bucket list, and after three years of working full-time, I felt ready for a change of scenery and a new challenge. In my mind, the possibility of getting into NYU was slim to none. It was my dream school, full of prestige. Flash forward six months later and I received a letter from Cal Arts, the other graduate school that I applied to. The letter read, "We regret to inform you..." My heart sank. I didn't get in. In a matter of seconds, my dream of graduate school was put on the shelf. "At least I have a job," I thought. A few weeks later, I got a letter from NYU. I casually opened it, expecting nothing, and was suddenly surprised. "Congratulations! You've been accepted to..." Instantly, I started crying; a combination of happiness, surprise, and fear washed over me. I got into my dream school. I did it. But what was I going to do? Was I going to quit my job and move across the country? Leave my boyfriend and family behind? Not only that, but was I going to allow myself to get even further into debt?

NYU is a private school with a hefty price tag. The cost of my one-year accelerated program was $52,000. That was far more than my salary at my nonprofit job and a number that seemed incomprehensible to me. For the next several months, I kept thinking about it and weighing my options. I waivered back and forth frequently, never quite sure what I wanted to do. Everything felt so safe in LA. Moving to New York was a risk, financially. I'd have to let go of everything and start over.

Ultimately, I made the decision to go. I knew if I didn't ever leave home or go to grad school, I'd regret it. And I do my best to live a life without regrets. So I gave notice at my job and had "the talk" with my boyfriend. While I was relocating to New York, he relocated to Portland, Oregon, to attend school. Despite being across the country from each other, we agreed to a long-distance relationship while I was in school. Just two months after giving notice, I sold most of my belongings and took a one-way flight to New York to start my new life.

———•◦•———

Dear Debt,

I have welcomed you into my home for the last fourteen years. I have had many members of your family come to visit and in some cases even stay a long time. It all started with your friendly brother, Student Loans. He told me he would only be around for a couple years. He even said that I needed him if I wanted to go to school, graduate, and become a major success. Fourteen years later he is still staying at my house. He takes money from me every month in the form of payments; these include principal, a.k.a. the promise to leave, and interest, a.k.a. the promise to make my working days last 12,000 days.

That is just the beginning; I met your sister, Credit Cards, shortly after letting student loans enter my home. I dated your sister and to me she is one of the worst people I have ever met. Some people say there are good ones out there if you find the right one, but I have been damaged and beaten down by her—I don't think I will ever find the right one. It did not help that I didn't know how to treat a woman so early in my financial life, but she made things painful. She charged me a high interest rate, fees, and told me I had to pay at a certain time otherwise the interest rate and fees would go even higher. It was like when I would pick her up one minute late, she would make me feel guilty the whole time we were together and it would cost me.

You must have a lot of sisters because this is not the first or the last one I have ever met. Sometimes they are nicer, offering low interest rates, but they are all the same, eventually going back to the high interest rates and fees because they have me locked in. They know that nobody wants their sorry minimum payment of a relationship…or maybe it's that everyone wants their minimum payment relationship, but they don't really care.

I quit them altogether a couple years ago; I was through jumping from girlfriend to girlfriend. I held on to one and gave her extra money to go away. Finally it worked; your sister(s) left for good. Despite others saying how attractive she is, I refuse to date her. I found what I like to think is my new girlfriend, Cash. We have been getting along great. She doesn't expect things from me and she's not secretive or manipulative. She's honest and I can see myself being with her for a long time.

During my time with your sister, Credit Cards, I also came across your uncle, The Car Loan. I didn't see him until I was out of college, but man is he a talker. He saw that I needed a car and he had no problem showing me the most expensive car I could afford, a nice Mercedes Benz. He didn't even care that I wasn't making much money. He told me things to get me on board like "you worked hard throughout college," "you have been in the same car since high school," "you have a real job now," "get the car loan, that's what everyone does."

The good news about your uncle is that he did not stay long. I was able to sell the expensive car that he talked me into getting and I kicked him out, but not before hurting me with car maintenance, gas, insurance, expensive monthly payments, and loss of car value. To make matters worse, I used your sister to pay for all of these except the last one because I didn't have any Cash. I have not had your uncle in my home in over four years, and not having your uncle made getting rid of your sister that much easier. Funny how that works.

The last family member that is currently staying at my house is your child, The Mortgage. They say having a kid is a great thing and that kids are the good kind of debt. I'm not sure I agree. When you already have a whole family of debt staying in your house it makes caring for your child that much harder. They tell me that your child is going to grow up with us for thirty years, assuming I make all the payments on time. The good news is that I will not be raising your child for you; I am making extra payments on my own and even have come to an agreement with a couple other families to help pay off this debt. Only then can this child go out into the world on his own. If I have your child stay in our house for thirty years I'm not going to be able to make all of the choices I want, and I want to be able to live a debt-free life. I'm sorry Debt, that's just the way it is.

I've made a plan to kick out your friendly brother, Student Loans, in April 2015; he's just annoying. He won't go away. He's not hurting me financially, but I don't want him living in my home anymore. I have two of your children staying at our home, but I don't plan on them staying long. One will be gone in December 2016 and the other in July 2020. That's the day the home is really mine, the day I can kiss your family goodbye.

I don't plan on ever inviting your family to come visit again. I don't care if you write letters or send emails, advertise on my favorite website, or talk to me when I'm going to grab some Cash; the answer is a loud NO! Our time is soon to be over. I may have had some fun with your family, but it was short-lived.

The foolish thought that you would help me was my own fault. I should have known better. I'm sick of taking care of your family like it is my own. I'm ready to never see you again. It might not be tomorrow but I have plans to kick you out forever. Debt, I'm going to share my story with others so they know how terrible your family is and how you're dragging everyone down. I hope they will read this and realize, Debt, your family is the worst.

Gone Forever July 2020,
Even Steven Money

CHAPTER 2

Starting Over

I arrived in New York with one suitcase and nothing else. I didn't even have a place to live, so I ended up sleeping on a friend's sofa until I could find a room to rent. Three days after I arrived, I started my intense graduate school program. The financial aid office had originally offered me a total of $89,000 to cover the $52,000 tuition plus cost-of-living expenses, but I still owed money on my undergraduate student loans and didn't want to borrow the full $89,000. Luckily, I didn't have any credit card debt. In the end, I ended up borrowing an additional $58,000 to cover my tuition, books, and food. To pay for my rent, I hustled and worked three part-time jobs while going to grad school full-time.

I had a work-study job during the week at NYU, taught theater at an after-school program in Harlem, and worked as a resident assistant on the weekends at a ballet school. Luckily, I was able to do my homework at my weekend job, which made everything work. Juggling three part-time jobs, graduate school, and a long-distance relationship was tough. I hardly slept and worked my butt off, but it was worth it. Even though I still ended up borrowing a lot of money for my graduate degree, it could have been much worse. I mitigated the damage by working while I was in school to help pay for my living expenses.

Though managing all of my responsibilities was tough, I loved living in New York. I felt like I was meant to be there. I enjoyed my classes and had meaningful and engaging part-time work. I was making all the right moves to secure a job after graduation, or so I thought.

In May 2011, graduation day came. I was filled with so much hope, but also riddled with intense anxiety. The safety of being in school was about to end and I wasn't sure what my future would hold. One thing I knew, though, was that I owed *a lot* of money and going to my dream school and living in New York came at a cost. My loan payments would be due in six short months and I needed a job to pay them back, stat.

Though I didn't have a job lined up when I graduated, things started off on the right foot. I had several phone interviews and was getting call backs for second interviews. I was still working part-time, but knew that I needed a full-time job to pay back my massive student loans and also have benefits. For months I was on a nonstop merry-go-round of interviews. Looking for a job *was* my job, and I had one interview lined up after another. Each interview seemed to get me closer to a job, and several times I even had second and third interviews. But after feeling like I had each job in the bag, I would inevitably get a disappointing email saying that they hired someone else.

In a few short months, I went on over thirty interviews but had nothing to show for it. The final straw was a fourth interview I had with an organization, and being humiliated because I completely failed their "hands-on" test of building a robot with Legos. The job was for a program coordinator position, something I had a lot of experience in, and I had already aced the interview with the team and the executive director. This last test went so bad that I left the building in tears. There was no way I was getting the job—and I didn't.

After so many interviews that led nowhere, I began to feel defeated and my financial situation became increasingly more stressful. I began to think that NYU stood for "Now You're Unemployed." My part-time jobs barely covered my rent and I started to blow through my savings. The grace period on my student loans was coming to a close and my first payment would be due soon. Not only that, but my long-distance relationship was becoming more strained as the emotional toll of underemployment took its hold. I felt like my time was up. I couldn't stay in New York and pay back my student loans without a full-time job. After being on the interview merry-go-round, I was ready to get off and start fresh. Even though I didn't want to leave New York, I knew I could reunite with my partner in Portland and save some serious money on rent. My savings would go a lot further there and I could actually put some money toward paying off my debt.

After living in Los Angeles and New York City, I thought I'd be a big fish in a small pond in Portland. I thought it would be easy to get a job given my work experience and my degrees. But while Portland is a liberal, creative city, it doesn't have the arts funding that LA and NYC had. I struggled to find work in my field. I struggled to find any work at all. The first job that I got was as an administrative assistant making ten dollars per hour. It was hardly enough to get by, as it was part-time, so at the suggestion of a friend I went on food stamps to help cover my expenses.

I felt so low. Never in a million years had I imagined myself being on food stamps after getting a master's degree from NYU—I thought my degree was the pathway to success. Being on food stamps was a humbling experience and a situation I desperately wanted to get out of. Eventually, I was able to secure a slightly better paying job, making twelve dollars per hour as a temporary study abroad advisor. It was fun work, but the pay was only slightly better, and although I was working full-time, it was a temp job and didn't provide any benefits.

After living in Portland for a year and working only low-paying jobs with no career in sight, I started to loathe my situation. Unlike New York, I could hardly get any interviews in Portland, even though I spent all my free time sending out resumes. I felt overwhelmed with how much debt I had and just how little I was actually making. I felt like I had worked so hard for everything and did what I was supposed to, yet here I was with a master's degree from one of the best schools in the country and I could barely get by. Millennials get a lot of flak for being "entitled," but our generation was told our whole lives, "You can be anything you want to be if you just work hard." Many of us found out how untrue that was after the Great Recession, with many of us facing steep student loan balances and limited job opportunities. The old adage "to get a good job, get a good education" didn't apply to my generation.

After doing everything I could to improve my situation, I felt stuck, miserable, and overwhelmed. Crying for no reason became a daily occurrence. I didn't know who I was without a career, and I felt like I had no purpose. In previous jobs, I felt like I was helping people. Now, I felt like I was trying to find my place in the world and my huge debt load was holding me back. As things got more tense and stressful, I began going to therapy to sort out my feelings. For months I felt out of sorts, crying, feeling like I would never have a job again, and thinking I'd never get out of debt (as a theater major I have a penchant for the dramatic).

So, I did what any good Millennial who grew up in the age of the Internet would do and I went online to find answers to my problem. I discovered a whole new world: personal finance blogs. I fell in love with their helpful advice and felt inspired. Then, I had a crazy thought. What if I started a blog and documented my journey? In that moment, I decided to start my own personal finance blog about getting out of debt. I wanted and needed to create a space where I could turn the negative energy and emotions related to my debt into something positive—into something that would keep me accountable in the debt payoff process. I figured that I couldn't be the only one dealing with student loan debt, and having a blog would help me connect with others dealing with the same problem.

On January 3rd, 2013, I wrote my first post declaring that I wanted to pay off all my debt in four years. At the time I was only making twelve dollars per hour, and that goal seemed galaxies away and completely out of reach. But I was tired of being broke, depressed, and in debt, so I was determined to do whatever it took to get out of debt. Starting my blog, Dear Debt, changed my life and my career in so many ways. Taking that first step of committing to pay off debt and announce it to the world was scary, but it changed the course of my life in a very positive way. My blog kept me accountable to paying off debt and led to so many opportunities. Turning my pain into my passion gave me a purpose and helped me find a community to cheer me on. Not only that, but it led to a new career: writing about money. Through my blog, I was able to secure more opportunities and ended up paying off the last of my debt ahead of schedule, in three years instead of four.

Before, I thought I'd never get out of debt, but once I knew it was possible, I wanted to help others reach their goal of being debt free, too. There is so much more to life than making payments on your debt, and you deserve to keep every cent of money that you earn.

Dear (Deadbeat) Debt,

Get off your ass and get a life. You are a lazy mother f#ck^& and I'm sick of you! I work EVERY SINGLE DAY to support you and what do I get in return? Nothing! You think I don't notice that you are slowly depleting all of my money. You would rather pretend things are okay with us.

Well, I'm here to tell you, "I'm onto you." Your secrets are out of the closet. I am no longer hiding in the shadow of your terror. Someday soon, the joke will be on you. Find another sugar momma!

Love,
M

CHAPTER 3

I'm in Debt—Now What?

For many years, I simply paid the minimum on my debt and treated it like any other bill. It never occurred to me to pay more. It wasn't until shortly after I finished graduate school that I decided to get my financial life straight. I knew my first payment on my graduate loans would be due soon, so I decided to sign up for Mint.com, an online budgeting program that allowed me to track my income and expenses. Once I synced all of my bank accounts and loans, I saw the damage right there in black and white. At the time, I owed $68,000. I had already been paying my undergrad loans for nearly five years, and seeing how much debt I had amassed and how little income I earned sent me into a panic.

A few days after signing up for Mint.com, I deleted my account. I was in complete denial and didn't want to admit how much I actually owed. Just thinking about it made me breathe heavy and feel a pang of anxiety. Coming to terms with your debt can be similar to the five stages of grief. I was in complete denial about how much I actually owed, but eventually moved through anger, bargaining, depression, and ultimately acceptance. I knew that I couldn't just sweep my debt under the rug, and it wouldn't go away magically. If you're in debt, what stage are you in?

Denial:

- You don't know your total debt amount.
- You don't know your loans' interest rates.
- You don't know your monthly payment amount.
- You don't know payment due dates.
- You're in complete denial of debt's existence.

Anger:

- You have a deep feeling of anger toward yourself, others, and the system in general.
- You feel regret, blame, and feelings of irrational anger or jealousy.
- Your anger often comes through as resentment. You think to yourself, "I resent that my parents couldn't help me. Why do some people have it so easy? No one has problems like I do and no one understands!"

Bargaining:

- You try begging for some understanding or help from a higher power to make your situation better.

Depression:

- You think a solution will never come.
- You feel like you're drowning in debt.
- You're unable to comprehend your current situation and how you got here.
- You feel lonely, isolated, and don't know what to do to start improving your situation.

Acceptance:
- You find resolve and accept actions and consequences.
- You acquire knowledge.
- You work to find a manageable solution.
- You make progress.
- You feel empowered.

Once I got to the acceptance stage, I realized that I couldn't wait for a government bailout or some unexpected windfall in order to pay off my student loans. I had to do it all by myself. Coming to that realization can be tough, but also liberating. If you're in debt and ready to take action and not let your debt define your life, here are the steps you should take.

Step 1: Find out how much you owe.

The first step to creating a debt payoff plan (and often the most painful) is finding out exactly how much you owe. If you have federal student loans, log in to the National Student Loan Data System to retrieve information about your loans. If you have private student loans, you can typically find information on your credit report at AnnualCreditReport.com. If you have credit card debt, look at your statements and add up all the balances.

Step 2: Find out the interest rates.

One of the things that makes paying off debt so difficult is the interest that accrues. Interest is the money that you pay to your lender for the convenience of borrowing money from them. If you have federal student loans, you probably have fixed interest rates, which could be a blessing or curse depending on your situation. My undergraduate loans had a low interest rate of 2.3 percent, while my graduate loans had rates of 6.8 and 7.9 percent. With such high interest rates, at my highest debt load, I was paying eleven dollars per day in interest. Yikes!

You can typically find your interest rates for your student loans on the National Student Loan Data System or through your loan servicer. If you have credit cards, a mortgage, or medical debt, check your account statement or contact your servicer to determine your interest rates. Be sure to write down the interest rate next to each account balance. In addition, calculate your daily interest. This exercise can help you put your debt into perspective and illustrate exactly how much you are paying in interest. I was shocked when I found out I was paying eleven dollars per day, which amounted to over three hundred dollars per month. You can use the following formula to calculate your daily interest:

Daily interest = interest rate x principal balance ÷ 365

Let's say you owe $40,000 in student loans at 6.8 percent interest. Daily interest = 0.068 × $40,000 ÷ 365 = $7.45

That means you are paying seven dollars toward interest every day. Imagine what else you could be doing with that money!

Interest can often make it hard to get ahead, so understanding how much you are paying each day and each month can help you develop a plan, ideally where you are putting more toward principal and aren't just paying interest. Many student loan borrowers end up making minimum payments, which can disproportionately go toward interest.

Your student loan payments typically go toward any late fees first, then interest, and then principal. If your minimum payment is $275 and you're paying $250 in interest per month, it's going to be tough to make progress on your debt. Calculating your interest can help you see what payments you should be making in order to really conquer your debt.

Step 3: Debt Snowball or Debt Avalanche?

After you've identified how much you owe, located your interest rates, and calculated your daily interest, it's time to choose a debt payoff strategy. When you first start paying off debt, it's important to have a plan. Without a plan, paying off debt can seem like a daunting task, which will quickly deflate any motivation you have to actually pay off the debt. Not having a strategy in place can keep you in the denial phase. But having a plan can help you realize that debt is not forever, and that it's possible to be debt free. So often, debt feels like a lifetime sentence, but it doesn't have to be.

In personal finance, there are typically two types of debt repayment methodologies: the debt snowball and the debt avalanche methods. There is no "right way" to pay off debt, but here's a closer look at these two popular options.

The Debt Snowball

The snowball method, which is revered by personal finance guru Dave Ramsey, focuses on paying off your smallest balance first. So if you have credit cards, student loans, and a car loan, the first step would be to list all of your outstanding balances.

Example:
- Credit card debt: $8,000 at 14.9% interest
- Student loan #1: $21,000 at 6.8% interest
- Student loan #2: $6,000 at 7.9% interest
- Car loan: $10,000 at 4.5% interest

Using the debt snowball method, you'd focus on paying off the smallest balance first, while making the minimum payments on the rest. In this case, you'd focus on student loan #2 first. After that is paid off, you move to the next smallest, and so on.

The theory behind this methodology is that it allows for quick wins, which can help motivate you on your path to debt freedom. One of the biggest hurdles to getting out of debt is your motivation, and this strategy is often cited for its motivational factor because you start small and get bigger over time. If you're struggling with motivation when it comes to paying off debt, this may be the right strategy for you. The downside of using this method to pay off debt is that you will pay more interest over time.

The Debt Avalanche

On the other side of the spectrum, you have the debt avalanche method, which focuses on paying off the debt with the highest interest rate first, while making the minimum payments on the rest. I used the avalanche method to pay off my student loans. My graduate student loans were over $50,000 with an average interest rate of 7 percent, while my undergraduate loans were markedly smaller with an interest rate of only 2.3 percent. My high-interest loans were costing me eleven dollars per day in interest.

The avalanche method helps you save money by paying off the debt with the highest interest rate first. You'll end up paying less in total interest and more toward principal, which can help you get out of debt faster.

Example:
- Credit card debt: $8,000 at 14.9% interest
- Student loan #1: $21,000 at 6.8% interest
- Student loan #2: $6,000 at 7.9% interest
- Car loan: $10,000 at 4.5% interest

Given this example, you'd focus on paying off your credit card debt first, while making the minimum payments on the remaining loans. Once your credit cards were paid off, you'd move on to student loan #2, then student loan #1, and finally the car loan.

So, which option is best? There's no right or wrong answer. The debt snowball method is good if you need a motivation boost, whereas the debt avalanche method allows you to save money on interest. You can find free debt calculators online to figure out how much you will pay in interest over time with each option. My favorite, easy-to-use tool is unbury.us. Simply input your balances and interest rates and then calculate your payments and overall interest with the snowball and avalanche methods.

Aside from these common strategies, I recommend two off-the-beaten-path strategies to tackle your debt. The first method is to focus on the debt that pisses you off the most. Why? Because anger can be a powerful tool to inspire you to pay off debt quickly. Do you have credit card debt from a stupid purchase that you regret? Or from an ex-boyfriend that you hate? Pay off that debt first. You'll feel so much better once it's gone. The second method is about paying off the debt that will help you sleep best at night. Debt repayment can be filled with anxiety, so pay off the debt that will help you sleep easier and be happier.

In the end, it's important to do what makes sense for you. It can be easy to get into analysis paralysis, thinking that you have to choose a plan and worrying that you're not doing things the "right way." Do it your way, but just do it. If you find that your strategy isn't working, try something else, but just keep going. The road to debt freedom is paved by small, simple steps, one foot in front of the other. Keep walking, and don't give up.

----------◆●◆----------

Dear Debt,

You are my noisy neighbor upstairs who blasts his terrible metal at 4 a.m.
You are the gum on my shoe.
You are the spinach in my teeth.
You are those last 5 lbs.
You are that zit on my nose.
You are Monday morning.
You are the black veil over my thoughts.
You are the stranger sitting a little too close.
You are the smell of rotting food.
You are the scars on my body.
You are the passive aggressive coworker.
You are the dust bunnies hiding in the closet.
You are the rats among trash.

You are prejudice.
You are Santa Claus.
You are a sinking ship.
You are the breakup that still hurts.

-M

CHAPTER 4

---·---

Which Debt Should You Pay Off First?

Debt can feel like a huge weight on your shoulders, especially if you have multiple loans with varying balances and interest rates. While I don't believe that a student loan is "good debt" (really, is debt ever good?), some debt is worse than others. Some debt, like student loans, can be leveraged in the form of a degree to get more opportunities that offer you a return on your investment. Not only that, but federal student loans offer flexible repayment options compared to some other types of debt. If you have various types of debt, consider which debt you should pay off first.

Credit Card Debt

If you have credit card debt, it's time to focus your energy on getting rid of it ASAP! Credit cards typically charge an average interest rate of 15 percent and up, making it easier to accrue a lot of interest. For example, if you carry a $1,000 balance on your credit card with a 15 percent interest rate, and you make minimum payments of

$25 each month, it will take you more than four years to pay it off and you'll pay nearly $400 in interest! Credit card debt should be a priority if you have different types of debt because the interest rates are so high. Not only that, but carrying a balance can affect your credit utilization, which could negatively affect your credit score. Your credit utilization is essentially how much of your credit limit you actually use. Let's say you have a $1,000 credit limit. Most experts recommend keeping your balance at 20 to 30 percent of your credit limit, which means you should only carry a balance of $200 to $300 at any time. The lower the amount you charge on the card, the better. Even if you pay off your credit card every month, you could be considered a risk if you're maxing out your credit limit.

If you have credit card debt, consider putting them away for a while and going on a cash diet while you pay down debt. There are multiple studies that illustrate how using a credit card can lead to increased spending. It's just too easy to swipe mindlessly and not really consider how much you are actually spending. Paying with cash hurts a little more...which is exactly what you need when trying to get out of debt.

Private Student Loans

If you couldn't cover your education-related costs with federal student loans, you likely took out private student loans. Paying off private student loans should be a top priority, as they offer fewer borrower protections than federal student loans. Private student loans usually don't offer income-based options or loan forgiveness options. If you are going through hard times, they also offer limited options to defer your payments.

In recent years, many private student loan lenders have gotten flak because of their business practices. Many private student loans require a cosigner, and if that cosigner dies, the borrower gets hit with an "auto-default." As if dealing with the death of a loved one isn't tough enough, you may suddenly receive a notice demanding immediate payment of the full balance of your student loans. If you have a cosigner on your private student loans, I recommend looking into a cosigner release, which can help you and your cosigner avoid a potential tricky situation in the future. Each lender is different, but typically they will want to see that you can handle the student loan payments on your own. They may ask for proof of income and require a certain amount of payments before you are eligible for the release. Unfortunately, the Consumer Financial Protection Bureau noted that in 2015, 90 percent of consumers that applied for a cosigner release were rejected. Ouch. This is one of the key reasons why it's best to prioritize your private student loans. They don't offer as much flexibility as federal student loans, and in some cases they may carry harsh consequences.

Federal Student Loans

As I mentioned, I don't believe there's any "good debt," it's just that some debt is worse than others. Federal student loans should be lower on your priority list as they offer many different types of repayment options. Depending on the types of loans that you have, you may be eligible for the following options:

- **Standard Repayment Plan:** Ten-year repayment plan, with fixed payments.

- **Graduated Repayment Plan:** Ten-year repayment plan, with payments that start out small and gradually increase, typically every two years.
- **Extended Repayment Plan:** Twenty-five year repayment plan, with fixed or graduated payments. Direct Loan and FFEL (Federal Family Education Loan) borrowers need to have more than $30,000 in student loans to qualify for this plan.
- **Income-Based Repayment:** Qualified candidates that prove financial hardship can have their payments capped at 10 to 15 percent of their discretionary income for twenty to twenty-five years, depending on when they took out the loans. After twenty or twenty-five years of consistent repayment, the remaining balance may be forgiven.
- **Pay As You Earn:** Qualified candidates that prove financial hardship can have their payments capped at 10 percent of their discretionary income for twenty years. After twenty years of consistent repayment, the remaining balance may be forgiven.
- **Revised Pay As You Earn (REPAYE):** Monthly payments are capped at 10 percent of the borrower's discretionary income for twenty to twenty-five years, depending on the loan. After twenty years of paying back undergraduate loans, the borrower's loans will be forgiven. Forgiveness is available after twenty-five years for those who have graduate student loans.
- **Income-Contingent Repayment Plan:** Payments are based on a variety of factors including income, family size, and total debt. Anyone with eligible federal student loans can qualify for this plan. Because it is a twenty-five-year repayment plan, any remaining balance will be forgiven at the end of the term.

The most cost-effective option is to opt for the Standard Repayment Plan and get your loans paid in ten years—but remember, you can pay more and get out of debt even sooner! Don't let the timeline convince you that you need to stretch out your payments. There are no prepayment penalties.

For those of you struggling to make your monthly payments, an income-driven plan may be a good option to consider. Under this type of plan, your monthly payments are based on a percentage of your income, and after making qualified payments for a period of time, your loans are forgiven. While it may seem like this is the best and easiest option to get out of federal student loan debt, it's important to know that under current tax law your forgiven loans will be considered taxable income. In other words, when your loan is forgiven, you could face a hefty tax bill. There are mutterings about this law changing, but as of now, forgiven federal student loans may result in a tax bill.

Federal student loans also offer the benefits of deferment and forbearance if you're going through tough times and unable to make payments. Depending on your situation, you may be able to postpone your payments for a few months or even a few years. Just be aware that depending on the type of loan that you have, interest may still accrue during your deferment. Talk to your loan servicer about your options and tell them if you are having trouble making payments. You must apply for these options first and get approved.

Aside from the numerous repayment plans, there is Public Service Loan Forgiveness for employees who work in the public sector. Under this program, you can get your loans forgiven after working for a qualified nonprofit or government agency for ten years and making 120 qualifying payments. The good news about this program is that your forgiven balance is not considered taxable income, so after ten years of working in the public sector, you can be debt free!

Car Loans

Cars are interesting because they depreciate as soon as they're driven off the lot, and they will never be worth their original cost. Because cars lose their value so quickly, you'll want to focus on getting rid of these monthly payments ASAP. Between your car payments, insurance, gas, oil changes, and repairs, cars can be an expensive liability. If your car loan is outrageous, you may want to consider downsizing your vehicle to something more manageable. If you live in a metropolitan city, you may want to consider ditching your car altogether. I've been car-free since leaving Los Angeles and have loved it! I don't have to worry about car payments, costly maintenance, parking tickets, insurance, or any unexpected repairs. I estimate that I save roughly six thousand dollars each year by not having a car. If you want to ditch your car altogether like I did, consider these options to help you stay mobile.

- **Your own two feet!** I walked nearly two miles to work for over two years. It was great exercise!
- **Biking:** When I had a longer commute, I'd ride my bike. Once again, great exercise.
- **Car2Go:** This service has been a game changer for me. Using Car2Go, you pay by the minute to rent a car and you can use it one way, instead of round trip.

- **Uber or Lyft:** These ride-share titans make it easier than ever to get where you need to go. If you need a ride here and there, these are your go-to options.
- **Getaround:** You can rent cars on the cheap hourly or daily using Getaround, which allows users to rent out cars they aren't using.

For those who can't go without a car, pay off your car loans quickly and drive safe! Any accidents or speeding tickets can quickly hike the cost of insurance. In addition, use a site like GasBuddy.com to find the cheapest gas in your area.

Medical Debt

Your health is one of your most precious assets. An unexpected illness or emergency can cause you to incur substantial medical debt. While having medical debt can feel like salt on a wound, there may be a way to get your medical debt lowered. Talk to the hospital or medical practitioner to see if there are any flexible repayment options. In addition, there may be special programs for low-income patients.

A few years ago, I unexpectedly ended up in the emergency room...and I was uninsured. This was before the enactment of the Affordable Care Act and I was so worried about my bill. A four-hour visit to the emergency room resulted in a bill of $1,600. That was more than I was making in one month at the time. When I received my bill, I called the number on the invoice and asked if there was any way they could reduce the bill. In fact, they did have some options available, but I'd have to send over a few documents to see if I was eligible for partial or full forgiveness. I filled out the application and sent over nearly all of my personal data, including bank statements, tax returns, pay stubs, and receipts. It felt invasive and uncomfortable, but two months later I received a notice that my bill was forgiven 100 percent! I cried happy tears that day.

Medical debt can be scary and frustrating, but remember, everything is negotiable. If you have been hit with a huge bill, call your medical provider to discuss payment plans, forgiveness options, and lowering your potential interest rate.

Dear Debt,

This is getting old. Real old. I've turned into the old nag and you the grouchy old man. Isn't this exactly what we didn't want? We used to be friends, but let's be real— now we're just roommates.

I remember the days when you used to excite me. I wouldn't dare think of being with anyone else. Our love was "forever." But what is forever, anyway? Forever is a commitment you make; a choice. But you haven't been in it to win it for years. And I'm done. I wish I could say I was angry, because then at least I'd feel something, but quite frankly I'm just bored to tears.

I'm sick of talking about the same things over and over again. That same joke you always tell sucks. It's still not funny. I realize we have nothing to talk about these days because you don't DO anything. The key to success in any relationship is growing together and you've shown me that you just aren't available. Your interest compounds in some ways, but I'm left alone feeling like I just got robbed. What about me?

I hate to say it but your friends are just as bad. They think I don't know what you are up to when I am not looking.

Shenanigans.

Don't try to pull that $hit on me. You should know better. But you're a cowardly man-child who wouldn't know a good woman if she slapped you in the face. So consider yourself warned. One day you'll wake up and I'll be gone. For good.

-M

CHAPTER 5

You Are Not Your Debt

Money is one of the last taboos. Many of us would rather discuss how many people we've slept with than share the intimate numbers of our income or debt. It's because of the taboo nature of money that many of us are left ill-equipped to take control of our finances and deal with our debt. Debt can feel like a dirty word, and being in debt can fill you with feelings of shame and guilt. The emotions related to debt can be so consuming and overwhelming that they actually detract us from making progress toward paying off our debt. For so long, I was embarrassed by my debt. I carried it around with me, feeling like I had nothing to show for it. I went to my dream school and for what? I found myself struggling to find work, anxious about my nearly $1,000 monthly debt payments. I felt so low. I didn't feel comfortable talking to anyone about my debt. It made me feel anxious, depressed, fearful, and angry. Every purchase I made became an excruciating experience. Each month when I'd log into my account to make a payment I'd feel sick when I saw how much I still owed and how much of my payment was being eaten up by interest.

Because I chose to go to a fancy private school and had all of this debt and not a viable career to pay it back, I felt embarrassed most of all. I thought I followed the tried-and-true formula of success: work hard, play nice, and go to school. Not being able to find a job and being mired in debt felt like a new low. But after grappling with all of my emotions, one day I had an epiphany. I am not my debt. Uttering that simple statement had a profound effect on me. For years, I conflated my worth with my debt—my net worth was my self-worth, which meant my self-esteem was deep in the negative. But then I finally realized that all of the mistakes and missteps that I took to get into debt didn't have to define me as a person. It didn't mean I was a bad person. It didn't mean I was less than.

If you're dealing with debt, acknowledge that fact, but don't let it define you. Commit to overcoming it, not letting it defeat you. When you define yourself by your debt, you are selling yourself short and giving up your power. Debt does not have to be a forever thing and you are worth so much more than your debt.

Dear Debt,

I really can't stand your ugly ass. You weigh me down and cause me unnecessary stress. I think about you all the time when there are much better things to be concerned about. I wonder what I'll feel like on that special day when you will no longer exist in my life. The day your ugly ass can no longer call a place in my life home, will be the best day ever.

You lured me in with your enticements when I was only a baby. Fresh outta high school without a dollar to my name, you made me fall in love with you. I'll admit you had me whipped. Had me acting a fool over you. I loved you hard. You supplied all of my young needs. I was so eager to use you—never thinking of how I would pay ten times over for enjoying the temporary pleasure you provided.

I had no protection from you. I didn't know what I was getting myself into because I wasn't taught any better. In school we're taught to protect ourselves from unwanted pregnancies and diseases, but taught little about your ugly ass and how you can taunt us for decades if we don't take precautionary measures against you.

If I'd known what I was up against, I could have prepared mentally and financially. The income from my summer internships wouldn't have been wasted on providing you with your minimum monthly maintenance. I could have invested that money and watched it grow. I could have practiced the art of self-discipline. Instead, I'm trying to teach my 31-year-old-self tricks I could have learned years ago.

Half of the stuff you brought into my life I didn't even need. College students didn't need the latest from Victoria's Secret, Foot Locker, or Macy's. The only thing I needed was my mind and the education which I set out for.

Anyway, I'm tired of your ugly ass stalking me. I have become exasperated by your ability to multiply even though we aren't cool like that anymore. I want you to leave me alone and I've decided to do something about you. I'm coming for you. I'm an ex-lover scorned and I can't wait to annihilate your ass. The clock is quickly winding down on you, so I hope you're prepared. You can't do this to me anymore. I will not let you have any more of my present or my future.

I hope you're prepared to say goodbye. The day is coming quickly and there isn't a thing you can do about it. Got any questions? I hope not because I'm no longer answering to you.

Deuces.

This letter was written by Latoya.

CHAPTER 6

How to Overcome Debt Fatigue

When you first commit to paying off debt, it feels like you've taken one big step in the right direction. You feel motivated, inspired, and ready to rock! But after a while, that feeling can wane and wither away. After feeling so motivated and making consistent payments for a while, you may be hit with the dreaded *debt fatigue*. Debt fatigue is when you are sick and tired of paying off debt and you've lost your motivation. I've already mentioned that motivation and mindset are huge players in your debt repayment and can make or break your success. When debt fatigue hits, you can be thrown off-track and your progress can be derailed.

If you can pay off your debt quickly, it's best to do so in order to avoid debt fatigue. However, if you are planning to repay your debt over several years, debt fatigue may be inevitable. When I first became committed to paying off debt, I felt a surge of motivation, but after months of putting my nose to the grindstone and realizing I would have years (at least four!) left of repayment, I felt deflated. I was tired of paying off debt and felt so over it. So much of my income was going toward debt and it started to feel like I'd never see the end of it. Over the nine years it took me to pay off all my debt, I experienced debt fatigue a handful of times and learned tips and tricks to overcome it. If you're feeling like you're sick and tired of paying off debt, here's how to combat debt fatigue.

Understand Your Why

Debt fatigue can make you lose sight of your goals, so it's crucial to remember why you want to get out of debt in the first place. For me, getting out of debt meant traveling more, having less stress, and building wealth. In order to stay motivated, I created a secret Pinterest board about my life after debt. The board included places I wanted to travel to, new experiences I wanted to have, etc. I changed my computer desktop to pictures of exotic places to remind me what I was working toward. I put post-it notes showing my debt balance on my debit and credit cards so I would always be reminded of how much I owed.

Getting out of debt doesn't mean much unless you understand why it's important to you and what being debt free means for your future goals. Start by writing down why getting out of debt is important to you. Maybe it means quitting your job, traveling more, or saving money to purchase a house. Whatever it is, write it down and put visual reminders everywhere you can: on your computer, fridge, credit cards, bathroom mirror...anywhere. To get out of debt successfully, you have to commit and take action. Hitting a plateau can hinder your progress, so having these reminders can help propel you to action when you're feeling exhausted by the weight of your debt.

Change Up Your Strategy

When you're making payments toward debt each and every month, it can feel like you're just going through the motions. It feels like you'll never get out of debt. But that's not true! Try changing up your strategy. For example, if you're focusing on paying off high interest debt first (the debt avalanche method), instead focus on paying the smallest balances first (the debt snowball method). If you're focusing on the smallest balance first, start focusing on the highest interest balances instead.

One last thing you can do is to focus on saving more money instead of just paying off debt. While paying off debt is a guaranteed return on your investment, saving can be just as fruitful. Sometimes seeing more cash in your account can give you the boost needed to keep going. Changing your strategy can give you a fresh perspective to pay off debt.

Treat Yourself

Some people think that when you're paying off debt you should never travel, never go out to eat, and pretty much never have any fun. I am not that person. I know firsthand that kind of behavior is not sustainable, especially if it will take you several years to pay off your debt. Instead, start budgeting for some planned fun and turn it into a game. For example, for every $1,000 you pay off, go out to dinner and celebrate. When you pay off $5,000 get a massage and when you pay off $10,000 go on a day trip. When you set up a system for rewards, you're not just paying off debt aimlessly, but also working toward something fun as well.

Aside from the debt payoff benchmarks, you can have frugal fun day-to-day by hanging out with friends, occasionally getting a nice latte, or curling up with a good book. Paying off debt doesn't have to mean complete and utter deprivation. Sure, you have to cut back, but it doesn't have to be an all-or-nothing strategy. Doing so can quickly backfire, like a crash diet.

Getting out of debt is hard work, so make sure to schedule mini rewards and some fun for yourself. You're worth it! Using these strategies you can beat debt fatigue and keep going, even when it feels like all you want to do is give up.

Dear Debt,

You are a selfish lover. You always come first and have no interest in my needs. You're only INTERESTed in yourself and stroking your own ego. Although you come with a big package, you don't know how to use it. When we got together so many years ago I thought you were just a fling. You were hot, and I thought you made me smart, look cool, and feel important. I meant something because of you. Now after all these years I see you were simply filling a void for me. I didn't believe in myself, so I got with the first cute, smart guy that looked my way.

I'm done with this crap. I'm tired of your empty promises. After seven years, we haven't progressed past friends with benefits. Seriously, what is this? Shouldn't we be married with kids by now? I've wasted my youth on you.

But you won't get the last of me or the best of me. I'm moving on to someone new, babe. When you find this letter, I'll be gone and don't come looking for me. The affair is over.

Your Friend,
Melanie

CHAPTER 7

Starting Your Journey Out of Debt

Getting into debt is easy, but getting out of debt is another story. If it were simple, everyone would do it. There's a reason why so many people are stuck in debt: getting out of debt requires a level of commitment and perseverance that can be tough to sustain. The mere idea of it can be overwhelming. The first step is making the commitment to get out of debt by saying, "Yes, I will do this, no matter how long it takes, I will get there." Taking that first step can be intimidating—the beginning is always the toughest. You're walking down an unknown path. It can be scary and requires you to change everything and try something new. The commitment to change and overcome a big, audacious goal like getting out of debt can mean changing your lifestyle, your mindset, and everything you thought you knew. It means being bold, even in the face of rejection or failure. It means continuing on, even when you want to give up.

Before you get overwhelmed by the path ahead, remember that everybody has to start somewhere. Think about all the successful people that you admire. At one point, they were where you are: at the beginning. Nobody starts out perfect or having all the answers. Doing anything big and bold, like getting out of debt, is a process of trial and error. You learn as you go, but the key is to keep going, even when it's hard. The act of beginning is an act of courage. Beginning is the opposition of fear and complacency. Let's face it, it's easy to be scared of having big goals like getting out of debt. Many times I wish I could have been like my friends that didn't care about their debt or simply swept it under the rug. Instead, I became consumed with my debt. I wanted it gone *yesterday.* Committing to paying off $81,000 was the hardest thing I've had to do and was a huge goal at the time. It wasn't easy, but you know what? All things worthwhile in life aren't easy. And being debt free is worthwhile! Don't let the starting line intimidate you because your peers are half a mile ahead. Start where you are, in your own time, as best you can. Let the fear of failure fuel you. Keep trying, even if you stumble. You build confidence through trying. The way to get out of debt is by taking one step at a time. Know there will be struggles and setbacks—that is part of the process, but it doesn't mean you should give up. Start where you are and keep going.

Think about what being debt free means to you. How will not having debt payments each month change your life? Sure, you'll free up a lot more money, but what will you be able to do with that money? Money doesn't mean a thing without context, so it's important to think about how you want to use money as a tool to make your life easier, more enjoyable, and more illustrious. For me, getting out of debt meant freedom and travel. It meant letting go of guilt and being able to grow my business. If you are unsure what being debt free will mean to you, think about all the ways that debt is currently holding you back. Is debt forcing you to stay at a job you hate? Is debt taking away all your extra money, so you have none for yourself or your future? Is debt stressing you out and ruining your health? Is debt holding you back from having a child or buying a house? Being in debt can defer our dreams and delay our adulthood in so many ways. Instead of getting stuck in that place, let it motivate you to reach your goals. Once you're debt free, you'll be able to use that same motivation that got you out of debt to achieve all of your other goals.

———————

Don't Give Up Hope, Even When the Road Is Hard

When you want to give up
Throw in the towel
Be done with this shit
Cry in the corner
Scream in a pillow
Don't give up hope.

Believe in yourself.
Believe in possibilities.
You may not see it now; the hard work you are doing.
It doesn't make any sense does it? Why would it?
It's nonsense and all sense.
Life is beautiful, even amidst the chaos.

If you are buried in debt, take a deep breath. Be grateful you are alive.

Enjoy food that keeps you nourished. The roof over your head.

If you hate your job, be grateful you have one, and try to get out.

If you don't have a job, keep looking. Have faith. Things change.

It's all cyclical.

But most of all, don't give up hope.

If you are single and lonely and can't find love, enjoy your friends. Enjoy your hobbies. Enjoy freedom in your solitude.

If you are in a partnership, say "I love you" every day. Remember why you fell in love. Savor that moment. Replay it in the cinema of your mind.

But if you feel like your world is falling apart, don't give up hope.

It's a test. Life will throw many of them at you. It might shake you to the core, change your outlook.

It might make you wary, tired, or depressed.

Just don't give up hope.

If it's really bad, please seek help.

You are not alone.

If you dream of better days, keep those dreams alive.

This is only temporary.

If you are living your dreams, give back to others who need some support.

We need you.

You can do it.

You can get out of debt. You can find the love of your life. You can move where you want. You can find a different job. You can make money at your passions. It is all possible.
The broken record is just that, broken.
Put on something new.

Even if everything is telling you, "No," fight to say, "Yes." Fight for what you believe in. It's your life, nobody else's. You have to want it.
Just don't give up hope.

CHAPTER 8

———•—•———

Resources to Help You Ditch Debt

When you make the decision to get out of debt, you may experience an initial surge of excitement and momentum. But when you look at your balance and the road ahead, you can quickly get deterred. Getting out of debt is no easy feat and it's even harder because debt is either not talked about at all, or it seems so commonplace that many people write it off as "good debt." But if you're committed to getting out of debt, having the right tools and resources to help you can make or break your success. Here are my favorite tools to help you pay off debt and stay motivated.

Student Loan Hero
www.studentloanhero.com

If you have student loans, you know how confusing it can be to keep track of your balance, interest rates, etc. I didn't even know exactly how much I owed when I graduated with my B.A. and I was shocked to find out how much interest had accrued while I was in school.

If you're looking to get your student loans under control, consider signing up for Student Loan Hero. Founder Andy Josuweit struggled with unhelpful loan servicers and confusing advice when he was trying to pay back over $100,000 in student loans. After getting fed up, he decided to take matters into his own hands and create a solutions-oriented system for student loan borrowers. Using Student Loan Hero, you can create a free account and see your loan totals and interest rates. Not only that, but Student Loan Hero will recommend repayment plans to help you get out of debt, and their free online calculators will show you how much you can save in interest. They also have great blog content that can help you get a handle on your student loan debt.

ReadyforZero
www.readyforzero.com

If you have various types of debt, ReadyForZero may be a good fit. ReadyForZero is a tool that illustrates various repayment methods and helps you create a plan to conquer your debt. You can track your debt repayment progress and find out what options will save you money over time. They also have a helpful "next steps" function that can guide you on your debt journey and what to do next, such as consolidating your loans, fixing your environment, and checking your credit score. Creating an account is free, and ReadyForZero also sends you fun emails each time you pay off a loan to encourage you to keep going. It's a fun way to be reminded that you're not alone and you have a community to back you up.

SoFi
www.sofi.com

When I graduated in May 2011, my graduate loans were at $58,000 with interest rates of 6.8 and 7.9 percent. Because of the student loan crisis, many people like me struggled with high interest rates on hefty balances. Out of this problem came a new solution: student loan refinancing. Through student loan refinancing, you essentially apply for a new loan at a better interest rate. You will then pay off all of your old loans, and be left with one monthly payment at a new, potentially lower interest rate. If you can refinance your mortgage to get a better rate, why not refinance your student loans, too? I wish I would have known about refinancing sooner. For student loan borrowers in the thick of repayment, refinancing may be a viable option if you have good credit and secure employment.

There are a lot of companies that offer refinancing, but SoFi is leading the way when it comes to student loan refinancing. The downside to refinancing, however, is that you will be assuming a private loan, effectively losing any federal student loan protections such as income-based repayment or student loan forgiveness. So, if you're looking to get your loans forgiven after being on an income-driven plan, or you're looking for benefits such as Public Service Loan Forgiveness, this is not the option for you.

Student loan refinancing may be the right fit if you:
- Have private student loans
- Have a strong credit score (typically 700+)
- Have steady employment

- Have federal student loans and plan to pay them off quickly, without opting for any benefits such as loan forgiveness or an income-driven plan

Payoff
www.payoff.com

The Payoff Loan™ is a type of credit card consolidation that may help borrowers simplify their payments and pay much less in interest. Instead of paying multiple credit cards with exorbitant interest rates, you'd pay one loan at a potentially better rate. Borrowers can get a Payoff Loan™ from $5,000 to $35,000 at fixed rates between 8 and 22 percent APR with a repayment term of two to five years (your choice). If you can get a better rate with Payoff than your credit card, this makes financial sense. You can fill out a quick application to receive your potential rate, with no impact on your credit score. If you find something you like, then choose an offer and receive the money in your bank account. Pay off those pesky credit cards, save money on interest, and simplify your bills.

An important note about refinancing: You have to be ready to get out of debt and do the hard work before you commit to consolidating or refinancing your loans. It's key to understand the root cause of why you got into debt in the first place. Was it an income issue? A spending issue? A cash flow issue? Did you have to borrow for school? It's important to know why you got into debt in order to get out of it. No consolidation or refinancing plan will work if you keep borrowing as a Band-Aid.

10 Blogs to Help You Get Out of Debt

1. The College Investor: TheCollegeInvestor.com
2. The Debt Myth: TheDebtMyth.com
3. Financially Blonde: Financially-Blonde.com
4. Enemy of Debt: EnemyofDebt.com
5. Blonde on a Budget: BlondeonaBudget.com
6. And Then We Saved: AndThenWeSaved.com
7. Budgets Are Sexy: BudgetsAreSexy.com
8. Well Kept Wallet: WellKeptWallet.com
9. Dream Beyond Debt: DreamBeyondDebt.com
10. Dear Debt: DearDebt.com

Dear Debt,

The end is near. I see myself breaking free from your chains in the not-so-distant future. While my heart yearns to break free from you and get my life back on track after you've bankrupted me, I'm scared. I'm scared to be alone. You were my first love right after college. You made me feel important, like I was worth something.

Everything I've ever known in this life, I've known it with you. Who am I, if not standing in your shadow? After nearly a decade together, I don't know who I am without you. Debt, you were there to get me through college. You helped me go to my dream school. You pushed me harder and harder, just so I could keep up with you. You've pushed me so hard that I thought I might never come back. But I also don't want to focus only on the bad stuff. I know you've given me many opportunities, too. Without you, I might have never gone to college. I wouldn't have the career I have today.

It's all because you pushed me, for better or worse. But it's my time now to figure out who I am without you. I don't love you anymore, and quite frankly, I don't need you anymore either. I'm scared to be without you, but this is a path I must walk alone.

It's over,
Melanie

PART 2

How to Save Money So You
Can Rock Debt Repayment

CHAPTER 9

---·---

How to Avoid Spending Temptation by Knowing Your Spending Triggers

When it comes to personal finance, there are two schools of thought when it comes to money: spend less or earn more. Spending less sounds simple enough, but it can be a tough adjustment for anyone who's used to a certain lifestyle or has set behavioral patterns. Not only that, but the temptation to spend is everywhere you look. We are inundated with a barrage of ads on our phones, computers, televisions, and billboards. If you are trying to spend less but having a difficult time changing your habits, here are five ways you can avoid spending temptations.

1. Unsubscribe from shopping lists.

We live in the digital age where everything we want is at our fingertips. It's both a blessing and a curse to have everything available to us in a few short clicks. After years of shopping online, attending events, and signing up for various activities, I bet you get a lot of emails. I'd also wager to guess that during Christmas, New Year's, Valentine's Day, and nearly every other holiday, you get about a hundred emails exclaiming the virtues of a once-in-a-lifetime sale that's coming. Am I right? While it may be tempting to jump on the 24-hour sale, it could lead you down a slippery slope. Why? Because a sale is not an excuse to spend. If you weren't going to buy it before it went on sale, why do you need to buy it now? To help avoid temptation, unsubscribe from all shopping-related email lists. You can use a free service like Unroll.me or Unlistr.com to quickly unsubscribe from any unwanted email subscriptions and keep your inbox temptation-free.

2. Turn your motivation into vision.

One way that I was able to curb my temptation to spend was by utilizing a simple trick. I wrote my debt total on a post-it note and attached it to my credit and debit cards. Every time I wanted to spend money, that's the first thing I saw, and I was instantly dissuaded from making a mindless purchase. Having a visual reminder of what you're working toward can help you avoid temptation.

3. Carry cash for spending-trigger situations.

Let's face it, we all have spending triggers that, given the right circumstances, encourage us to spend. Spending triggers are certain environments or emotional situations that lead us to spend, even on an unconscious level. For some people, a spending trigger may be going to the mall. For me, it's when I'm stressed out and tired. When I feel exhausted, money seems like an afterthought—a tool that can be used to make me feel better by going out to eat or socializing with friends. Of course, that is reasonable to an extent, but I can't afford to spend money every time I'm having a bad day or didn't sleep well the night before. It's crucially important that you understand your spending triggers and how to combat them. Remember that personal finance is not just about numbers; it is largely affected by your behavior and mindset.

Because I know that I tend to spend more when I'm overwhelmed or exhausted, I've implemented techniques to help me relax. In addition, I've worked to be proactive rather than reactive in life. Because I like to spend money on restaurants, I make it a point to always have food in my house and not wait until the crisis moment, where there is nothing left and I am forced to go out because my stomach is calling.

Once you know your spending triggers, leave your credit cards at home and use cash when you are in a situation where you might be encouraged to spend. Some people can't go into a mall without buying *something*—and if this applies to you, then I suggest avoiding the mall altogether or at least carrying a set amount of cash, so you don't go overboard. Carrying cash in these situations can help you budget and keep spending under control.

4. Ask yourself important questions.

Spending money is easy. If you want something, you can get it now and pay for it later. And that's why so many people are in debt. In order to get out of debt, it's key to rein in your spending and practice delayed gratification. Before you make a purchase, ask yourself the following questions:

- Do I need this?
- Does this make my life better?
- Is this worth the cost?
- What else could this money be used for?
- How will I feel about this purchase tomorrow?
- Do I already have something like this?

Answering these questions can help you think realistically and make an informed decision, rather than one based on emotions and spending triggers.

5. Create new habits.

Many of us tend to have set behavioral patterns when it comes to spending. In order to spend less and change your patterns, you have to create new habits. When I start to feel the desire to go out and spend money, I look up a fun recipe and experiment in the kitchen instead. When I feel like I just want to have fun, I go for a long walk instead and enjoy the simple things. I'm not saying that you shouldn't spend money on fun—quite the contrary. You want to spend money when it matters, not just because it's a habit or an emotional spending trigger. Think about those situations where you feel most compelled to spend money. What could you do instead that would feel equally as rewarding? It might be tough at first, but with any behavioral change, it gets easier over time.

If you want to commit to spending less, these five tips will help you manage your money and gain control over unnecessary spending.

Dear Debt,

How many seconds, days, and months do we have left together? You know you're on your way out and you're trying to test me. You want to make things hard for me. You want to see me squirm as I try to stay strong and get rid of you. You keep playing mind games with me, but I know you are just messing with me, because you're the one scared of being alone.

I won't deal with your crap any longer. I don't care what you throw my way in the next few months because I'm kicking you out. Even if it's the hardest thing I've ever had to do. I am saying no to the depression you cause me. I am saying no to the anxiety and fear you have instilled in me. I know I'm worth so much more than you ever had me believe. You did a good job of convincing me I was worthless, but I've gotten smarter.

If there's one thing I know about you, it's that you're sneaky. You like to play tricks. But I'm done with playing games. You are a man-child and need to grow up. I am older and wiser and I have changed, but you're still the immature child I met when I was seventeen.

It's time for me to move on and experience real life. Real adulthood. Not some stunted adolescence.

Good riddance.

CHAPTER 10

---·---

How to Be a Frugal Friend
Without Being Rude

You're in debt, but that doesn't mean you have to say no to having a social life. It took me years to figure out how to find the right balance. For so long, I would either reject my friends' invitations or I would grin and bear it and feel uncomfortable blowing my budget. It sucks to feel like you have to either stay at home and be a bore or go out with friends and spend more than you should.

Luckily, I've been able to crack the code and have found out how you can be a frugal friend without being rude. Yes, it's possible to save money and not insult your best friends. This is a key part of the debt repayment process. Just because you're paying off debt doesn't mean it's the end of your social life completely. It just means that you have to make some adjustments. Use the following tips to rock your debt repayment, while still having fun with your friends.

Initiate the Invitation

This one is easy, yet it took me so long to realize that this one powerful switch can change everything. The key to being a frugal friend is to initiate the invitation, with terms that align with your budget. I tend to invite friends over for dinner at my place, or out for happy hour. I also enjoy going out for walks, hanging out in the park, or going out for coffee or tea. All friendships are different, but those are my frugal standbys and they show that I want to spend time with my friends, without spending a lot of money.

Be Honest and Upfront

Sometimes honesty really is the best policy, and when it comes to going out with your friends, let them know about your big audacious goal of being debt free. It can also serve as an opportunity to bond over finances and shared goals. Your friends can serve as much needed accountability partners and support you on your debt journey. Not only that, but they'll be more understanding if you have to decline an invitation because of your budget. I've found that if you're honest with your friends about your financial situation, they can meet you where you are. Letting your friends know about your goal of getting out of debt and cutting back is a way to set expectations and be clear about what you can and cannot afford. If you get invited to an event that seems out of your price range, you can respond with a polite, "That's a bit out of my price range right now," or propose something else altogether.

Know When It's Time to Say No

I learned the hard way that you can't say yes to everything. "No" is hard to say to friends, especially when you don't want to hurt their feelings or come across as rude, but saying no can save your sanity and your budget. If something doesn't feel right in your gut, say "no." If you feel like you will be uncomfortable or regret making a certain decision, the word "no" is a good bet. You can say no graciously and turn around and invite them to do something else at a later date.

Connect with Your Values

Friendship doesn't have to cost money. I'm the first to admit that I love going out with friends, but what I really love is the conversation. I can do that for a fraction of the cost when I get creative and host a potluck or invite people to my house. I also find going on walks with friends is a great way to stay active and catch up. True friends are based on so much more than activities, so if you're feeling strapped for cash, connect where it really matters.

You can be a frugal friend without being rude! Just be sure to set expectations, take initiative, and do what feels right for you.

---

15 Completely Free Things You Can Do For Fun

Let's face it, life is expensive. It seems like every day we are asked to spend money on something, whether it's rent, bills, food, a gift, etc. It's hard to feel like we have money left over for ourselves, or for any sort of fun. With a little imagination, and an appreciation for the simple things in life, you can do a variety of activities for absolutely no money. That's right: $0. Your wallet will thank you. Here is a list of fifteen totally free things you can do for fun.

1. Go to the park. These days, we spend too much time sitting while working on a computer. Get outside and explore! Parks are nice places to hang out and relax, and during summer months many offer free concerts.

2. Go to the library and rent a movie or check out a book. Who needs Amazon when you can get what you want for free?

3. Go to a local art walk. Many cities have art walks with local galleries open for viewing. It tends to be the first or last week of the month, but check your local arts calendar in your city.

4. Check out your local community center's event calendar. You can find free performances, lectures, and classes at your community center.

5. Take a nap. My personal favorite. Naps may seem like they are a call to your youth, but they feel just as good as an adult. Catch up on some much needed zzzz's and relax.

6. Volunteer to be an usher at a performance at your local theater. Contact your local theater, orchestra, or music venue and see if you can volunteer to be an usher. You could save anywhere from ten dollars to over a hundred dollars by volunteering while seeing a show!

7. Volunteer your time and give to the less fortunate. Giving back to your community is a great way to boost your mood and make a difference in the lives of others.

8. Have a dance party in your bedroom. Put on some sweet jams and rock out. Channel your inner Beyoncé. Turn up the speakers and dance like nobody's watching!

9. Take a relaxing bath. Unwind and relieve the stress of the day.

10. Meditate. Sit up straight, cross your legs, and with your eyes opened or closed, focus on your breathing. Do this for at least five minutes, but ideally for as long as possible. You will feel centered and relaxed. See where your mind goes and let it think freely.

11. Create a fort in your living room with some sheets and blankets and go "camping." You don't need a tent or time off from work.

12. Write in a journal. This is a great way to capture your thoughts, free write, and express yourself. You don't have to show it to anyone. Write whatever you want, for however long you want.

13. Go for a run or long walk in a new neighborhood. You can explore the scenery, boost your endorphins, and get fit.

14. Raid your fridge and come up with a new recipe. Some of the best things I've made came out of necessity. Necessity is the mother of invention, so you might come up with something delicious and new!

15. Read blogs about your favorite topic. I'm biased, but there are a ton of amazing blogs available for nearly every topic. Do you like personal finance? Look no further! Clothes? Star Wars? Gadgets? There are plenty of other blogs out there for that, too.

It's fun to go out and spend money from time to time, but it is possible to have fun and enjoy your life without spending an extra dime. Using a little creativity and innovation, you can transform almost anything into a free, frugal activity.

How to Score Luxuries for Less

When you comb through your expenses, look at how much you are spending on beauty and self-care. If you're a woman, that number could be quite high! You may be spending money on things like pedicures, waxing, massages, facials, manicures, and haircuts. Let's face it, all of those "little luxuries" add up. If you're working to get out of debt, you may want to hold off on some of those luxuries for a while in order to save money. Of course, I don't advise never cutting your hair, or not splurging just because you're in debt. In fact, I actually encourage spending money on little luxuries as part of your debt payoff strategy to avoid debt fatigue. While paying off debt, I'd get my hair cut once a year and also splurge on a massage. Those two services alone could easily cost nearly two hundred dollars with tip. Luckily, a few years ago I found the ultimate secret to saving money on these luxuries: beauty schools.

I found a local beauty school that offered a variety of cosmetic services at a serious discount. The beauty school offered haircuts for ten dollars, pedicures for twelve dollars, and facials for thirteen dollars. One day, I decided to treat myself and spend thirty-five dollars on all of the above services—and let me tell you, it was awesome! Now, you may have reservations about going to a beauty school. The students are still learning, and what if they mess up your precious hair? Don't fret! In my experience, they have veteran teachers working alongside advanced students in case there's any questions or guidance needed.

When I got my haircut, it took a bit longer than normal, but it was worth the cost savings for me. For a fraction of the cost of a salon haircut, I had a beauty day and felt refreshed and new. And no one else knew the difference!

After hitting the jackpot at beauty school, I wondered what other services I could get at a discount simply by going to a school. So I searched and found a local massage school that offered massages for twenty-five dollars. I picked up the phone and made an appointment. The massage ended up being the perfect treat and stress relief, and it saved me serious cash. I've seen massages go for sixty dollars to one hundred dollars per hour. Sure, it didn't have the relaxing ambience of a spa, but the massage itself was perfect.

In addition, I found that culinary schools offered gourmet meals as part of their test kitchens! One local school offered a three-course lunch for nine dollars.

By looking for local schools in your area, you can still indulge in the occasional treat and self-care day without breaking the bank.

———————•◦•———————

Dear Debt,

I don't think you've ever really loved me. After all these years, I'm haunted by what feels like a farce. Am I the butt of your joke? Is this a game to you? I wish we could go back to the way it was. I remember the honeymoon phase like it was yesterday. You made me feel complete and safe. I felt like I could do everything with you—like I was invincible. It was as if only you and I existed and we created this beautiful world around us where every-thing was perfect.

But the perfect life was wrapped in lies. It was only our imagination. Fake money, fake dreams, and fake lives. Fake, fake, fake. Phony. Liar. Failure. You've failed me, and I've failed you. We've disappointed each other. It's time to get our shit together. I'm too old for this.

I have to get the courage to leave. I have to stand up to you—and say NO. I will not allow this to happen. Not this time, not again. I can't pretend everything's okay anymore and go on like we used to. I just can't do it. The truth is screaming out of me. Those unwanted words are waiting for you to pick them up. Put me back together again.

I'm fragile and scared—I don't know what it's like to be without you. My whole adult life has been surrounded by you, Debt. Part of me wants to hang on, because you're all I know. What will I do without you? Who will I be without you? So many questions and not enough answers.

There are no answers.

There are only choices.

I am making a choice.

Goodbye,
Melanie

CHAPTER 11

The One Simple Mind Trick to Help You Start Saving Today

In order to rock your finances, paying off debt is the absolute crucial starting point. Aside from paying down debt, it's also important to save more cash. For the majority of us, saving can be tough. It may feel like a chore or feel like there's never enough money at the end of the month to actually save. You may also feel as if you have competing priorities and everything is trying to capture the attention of your last remaining dollars.

There is one simple mind trick to help motivate you to start saving. Think of it as being in debt to your future self. Your future wants to be taken care of better than your present, so it behooves you to start saving today. Every day that you don't save, you are losing out on interest that could be making you money instead of costing you money. You are cheating your money from the beauty of time—the power of compound interest.

How many times have you gotten yourself in a situation where you wished you had more money saved up? Hindsight is always 20/20, but this is a message from your future self. Save more. Yes, you. Why? Because life isn't perfect. Life doesn't go as planned. Things happen. Instead of panicking at whatever life throws at you, you need to be prepared for the unexpected.

Why This Trick Works

When I was working my way out of debt, I was so inspired. Every day, I'd find a new way to save or earn more money to put toward paying down debt. Everyone knows debt is bad, so it feels good to pay it down. On the other hand, saving can seem like a boring chore. This trick works because it shifts your money mindset: saving is no longer something you "should" do, but it's something you have to do. You don't want to default on your future self, do you? You don't want to deal with creditors, right? You don't want to work until you die or have a retirement that includes cardboard boxes and cat food, do you? I didn't think so. So get started today and save more. Make your savings rate just a little uncomfortable. It's good for you, I promise. Comfort zones are where progress goes to die, so get out of your comfort zone. When I was putting several thousand dollars each month toward my debt, I felt so uncomfortable. It felt wrong, yet oddly exhilarating to put so much toward debt. In order to get ahead, you must do what most people are not willing to do. You have to go above and beyond and stop the paycheck-to-paycheck lifestyle.

The thing about saving is that the money is still there. It doesn't go anywhere. It's just stashed away and ready for you, but it's not actually lost. Every time you see the balance in your accounts rise, you will feel proportionally less stressed. Conversely, when you have little to no savings, your stress levels can be astronomical. I feel like many people feel anxious about saving money because it feels like letting go of something tangible. But it's still there! And it will be yours, if and when you need it.

So, if you want to start saving, think about how much debt you are in to your future self. Think of all the years you owe someone else, working on their time just to make a dime. Think of the precious moments of your life that are taken away because of financial worry. There is a better way. And it starts with a commitment to save and to save more than you think you need. Your future self will thank you.

Most financial experts recommend saving at least 10 percent of your income. If you can, I recommend boosting that up to 20 to 30 percent—remember, the cash will be there if you need it. If you want to pursue early retirement, strive for saving upwards of 50 percent of your income.

On the other hand, if these percentages are simply not possible, commit to saving at least 1 percent of your income. Sometimes when you are broke and struggling, you need every dollar to get by and saving money seems impossible. If that's the case, save 1 percent of your income and strive to earn more money through side hustling. If you make two thousand dollars per month, save at least twenty dollars per month. It's not a lot, but it's more about creating lifelong habits that encourage you to save a portion of your income. Not saving means you'll end up working more for other people, living their life and not yours. You deserve to live a life you love, without financial worry and stress—and it can be yours, by taking the first step and starting to save a portion of your income.

Dear Debt,

High school reunions are filled with stories of people who knew each other in high school, liked each other, never took that next step, married the wrong person, got divorced, saw each other at the reunion, and voila! Flame rekindled. Or they go on Facebook, reconnect, and suddenly love blossoms. Well, that's never happened with you. Thank God.

I remember there was once a time when you and I co-habitated pretty peacefully. I used you. I thought you were convenient. Sure, there was the occasional hiccup when you'd refuse me when I was making a purchase, embarrassing me, making me use cash, but then you'd call me and tell me that our relationship had expanded, had grown deeper. You encouraged me to date your sisters, and that it was okay to have more than one lover in our relationship. The more cards in my wallet, the deeper our love.

Somewhere deep down, I knew our relationship wasn't sustainable. Like the brief summer fling that has a tempestuous passion but is, intrinsically, never meant to be, such was our relationship. However, few of those summer flings of passion are so parasitical. You, Debt, were a parasite, getting much more out of me than I ever got out of you. You told me that it was okay to live beyond my means. I was living in Germany, single, and young. When would I ever get a chance to travel like I could, and to make the memories that I did when I was in bed with you? "You deserve this lifestyle," you whispered. "Live a little. You'll get pay raises. You can pay me off later." I listened. It's hard to avoid that pillow talk when you're so deep in the throes of lust.

At one point, we broke up. I'd moved back to the States. I sold things. I had my combat pay. I had money in hand. I got rid of you. But, you kept calling. And I finally answered the call, and once I did, we reunited lustfully to make up for lost time.

Instead of saving up and preparing for graduate school, where I'd have no income except for summer internships, you told me that I was going to make a lot more money when I graduated. I could break up with you then, but we could have a wild time in those intervening three years.

Fortunately, I met another lover who was jealous. She never had debt. She was interested in a beneficial relationship between us, would take care of me when I was old, would love me unconditionally for as long as we were together, and didn't cause me to feel guilty about my relationship with her. She was someone whom I could actually marry, happily. But, she refused to let me have another lover on the side, so you and I had to break up. Sure, you sneaked back in the side door with your not-so-nefarious cousins, student loans and a mortgage, but even then, I realized quickly that despite the perceived benefits we were better off cutting off the relationship entirely.

It took ten years from the time that my now wife told me that I had to break up with you, (Not So) Dear Debt, before we became completely financially independent. It was hard work. It required sacrifice, although not nearly as much as you told me that it would require.

I have never looked back. I've never had a flame burning for you. It is an amazingly empowering and freeing feeling to know that we can choose the life we want, don't have to worry about money, and certainly will never be tempted to listen to your siren call.

The experiences we purchase with cash are much more enjoyable than any of the trips I took with you. Food tastes better when bought with cash than it ever did when you and I used to go to restaurants. Having no mortgage or student loan means no encumbrance of the soul, like I used to experience with you, your sisters, and your cousins.

You were the worst lover I ever had. It wasn't love. You were a parasite on my soul, lying to me all of the time about how good you were for me. I'm glad I had the affair with you. It taught me what to look for, what I wanted, what was important to me, and gave me a hunger to live a life without you. I'm never looking back. I'm stronger for our relationship, but I hope others never fall prey to your cute little charms, for underneath, you're simply one word: Medusa.

Not so much love,
Me

This letter was written by Jason Hull.

Top Websites to Help You Save Money

When it comes to spending money on things that I need, my goal is to never pay full price for anything. I'm always looking for ways to score a deal or shave a few bucks off the purchase price. Today it's easier than ever to save money. There are so many websites that can help you look for discounts or get cash back. Before your next purchase, check out these websites first, and remember to only buy things you need and were already planning on buying.

- **CouponFollow.com:** I personally love this site because it crowdsources coupon codes for your convenience. Be sure to look here before making your next purchase. If you want to make it even easier, you can download their *Coupons at Checkout* web extension to automatically have relevant coupon codes applied any time you make an online purchase.
- **Swagbucks.com:** When you shop through the Swagbucks portal, you accrue points called SBs. You don't even have to spend money to earn points. You can simply search the internet or take some of their surveys to accrue points. Swagbucks has helped me get free Starbucks and Amazon gift cards, among others.
- **Ebates.com:** If you want cold hard cash when you shop online, Ebates is the place to be. You can earn cash back on qualified purchases.
- **Groupon.com:** Whenever I want to go out to eat, I peruse the food and drink listings on Groupon first. I've found some pretty great deals when it comes to restaurants, and I've had nothing but positive experiences.
- **UPromise.com:** What if I told you that you could earn cash back to put toward repaying your student loans when you make certain purchases? Well, you can! Using UPromise, students, parents, and graduates can earn cash back on qualified purchases, which can be used for your education. Student loan borrowers can link their loans and get payments sent straight to them. Simply sign up for an account and register your debit and credit cards.

- **Goldstar.com:** Just because you are getting out of debt doesn't mean that you should never have any fun. I'm a firm believer of that. If you're looking for a night of arts and culture at a discount, check out Goldstar to see what's available in your area.

———————

Dear Debt,

I feel….
Trapped.
Stuck.
Barren.
Dry.

Everything I do, you are there watching me, judging me. I never knew guilt before I met you, and now the feeling lingers with me like a bad stench I can't wash out. Every penny I spend, all the work I turn down, consumes me with guilt. I am trying to find a balance, but I'm not sure how. I know things aren't right, but I don't know how to make both of us happy. I can't satisfy your insatiable hunger. These mind games have driven me mad. Who owns whom? Who is in charge? My life is on hold while I cater to your every whim. Dreams deferred, choices postponed, it's always, "not now, but later." Later feels like an eternity, but I guess I'll just have to wait.

Love,
M

PART 3

How to Earn More Money
to Pay Down Debt

CHAPTER 12

Why You Need a Side Hustle

Imagine that one day you go to work and you find out your position has been eliminated. There's no sugar coating it…you're out of a job. What are you going to do next? After having a moment of panic—and maybe a stiff drink—you have to face reality and come up with a plan. Getting another job won't happen overnight. While applying for jobs, interviewing, receiving an offer, and starting a job, you may be out of the workforce for at least a month. Even then, it may be a few more weeks before you receive your first paycheck. Traditional employment forces workers to rely on the hand that feeds them, and as soon as that is cut off, you're on your own and shit out of luck. Many Millennials, having come of age around the Great Recession, are already acutely familiar with the experience of being unemployed or underemployed. It's not fun.

That's why it's so important for everyone to have a side hustle. A side hustle is something that you can do to make money outside of your main job. Okay, you may be thinking, "Where will I find the time?!" That's why it's called a hustle, and you have to dedicate your nights, mornings, and weekends to it. In return, you'll get extra cash, additional freedom, and the ability to set your own schedule. Not only that, but you have the comfort of knowing that if you *do* lose your job, you'll have something to fall back on to make extra cash.

Over the years, I've become a side hustle queen because I realized one thing: You should never have all of your financial eggs in one basket. You would never just invest in one stock, right? So why would you invest in one job or one stream of income? It's not a good idea for your financial security. Diversifying your income is vitally important if you want to rock your debt payoff goals and secure your financial foundation. Through side hustling, you can pay off debt, build an emergency fund, and have some additional fun money.

How I Started Side Hustling

I've always been someone who likes to make a little extra money on the side. Just ask my parents. They were not so thrilled when I decided to sell their CDs at the Warehouse to make some extra cash while I was in middle school, but I loved the feeling of making money. I hustled on and off when I was younger, but got serious about it after graduating from New York University. I was teaching theater and also working as an administrative assistant, but I didn't make enough income to cover my rent, food, and student loan payments. I had money in savings, but I was determined not to touch it unless I absolutely had to. So, I thought to myself, "What can I (legally) do to make money this week?" I wasn't sure, so I went searching for answers.

I started with the "Gigs" sections on Craigslist. After scrolling through spammy ads and inappropriate offers, I finally found something that looked legit. "Hand out flyers for pet adoption event in Central Park—make $20 per hour, pay within a week." Jackpot! I applied right away and within a few hours I got a call telling me that I had gotten the gig. It was some of the easiest money I've ever made. I handed out flyers in Central Park to encourage passersby to go to a pet adoption event, sponsored by a well-known company. Essentially, I was a brand ambassador, a person who represents or promotes a company at a public event.

After the event, I was hooked. It was an easy and fun job for a theater-oriented extrovert who likes talking to people. New York City had no shortage of brand ambassador jobs, so I felt lucky to find my ultimate side hustle. I went on to work for brands like Columbia Sportswear, Starbucks, Mazda, and a few others. Being a brand ambassador helped me earn several thousand dollars on the side each year, which helped me keep my savings account intact and reach my debt payoff goals.

Why You Need to Make More Money

When I moved to Portland, Oregon to reduce my cost of living and live with my partner, I was underemployed, making twelve dollars per hour at a temp job. I was on food stamps and could barely pay for anything besides my bills. I had slashed nearly every item in my budget. I shared a studio apartment with my partner. I didn't have a car, cable, gym membership...none of that. The only way I could have cut back further was if I decided to move back home or start fasting. I had hit a plateau with my finances and debt repayment progress. I couldn't cut back any further.

My only option was to earn more money. So I went back to my trusty side hustle sidekick: Craigslist. This time, I also added the site TaskRabbit, which allows users to hire out tasks and gives people like me and you a chance to earn extra money. Since I was so displeased with the state of my income, I made it my job to find more gigs and earn more.

I once worked an early morning brand ambassador gig promoting a local bagel company—free breakfast! One time I worked overnight at what some may call an underground rave, selling water bottles to sweaty, inebriated dancers. As soon as I stopped looking only for a traditional nine-to-five job and started looking for side gigs, a whole new world opened up to me. I realized there were so many ways to make money! Now, more than ever, the sharing economy has democratized the process of making money. Anyone can start earning income with little to no resources.

Guide to Side Hustling

So you know that you want to earn more money, but what should you do? You want to do something that isn't boring and pointless, and something that works with your schedule. Ask yourself the following questions before choosing a side hustle:

- What are you good at?
- How much time do you have to devote to side hustling?
- What's the minimum rate you're willing to work for?
- Do you have a car?
- What will people pay you to do?
- What kind of person are you? Introvert or extrovert?

These questions are important to answer so that you can decide what side hustle may be a good fit for you. For example, I love being a brand ambassador, but I know that many introverts would sooner die than talk to strangers. Also, if you don't have a car, being an Uber driver won't work out. When thinking of which side hustles will be a good fit for you, it's key to look at the amount of time and resources that you have available. More importantly, you need to discover the sweet spot where your skills intersect with what others are willing to pay for.

One way to find out what you are good at is by taking an inventory of the comments, questions, and compliments that you receive. Are people always telling you that you're good with kids or pets? Are they always telling you that you have a knack for writing or making music? If you're constantly getting complimented or people are coming to you for advice, it's time to monetize that!

You are a creative, money-making machine and your talents are worthy of getting paid. One way to ensure that you always have a side gig is to find someone's pain point. In other words, what can you provide that makes someone's life easier or better? What can you offer that other people can't? You'll always find a gig if you can provide value.

List of Side Hustles

If you want to make extra money, here's a list of side hustles for you to try. If you don't see something that interests you on the list, make it up! Seriously, you can monetize anything. (Have you heard of the pet rock?)

My favorite side hustles:
1. Become a brand ambassador.
2. Work as a babysitter.
3. Enjoy furry friends as a pet sitter or dog walker.
4. Teach others as a tutor.
5. Write resumes and cover letters.
6. Become a grant writer.
7. Work as an Uber or Lyft driver.
8. Deliver groceries or takeout food.
9. Become a mystery shopper.
10. Become a beta tester for websites.
11. Get naked in the name of art as an art model.
12. Sell your art.
13. Work as a caterer.
14. Sell old CDs and books (but not this one).
15. Sell your unwanted clothes.
16. Do social media for companies/organizations.
17. Become a freelance writer or editor.
18. Volunteer to participate in medical research.
19. Donate plasma, eggs, or sperm.
20. Work as a coat checker.
21. Pour alcohol at private events, if you are certified.
22. Search the internet using Swagbucks.
23. Complete online surveys.
24. Become a consultant. You're an expert at something!
25. Clean houses.
26. Work as a handyman.
27. Be a TV or movie extra.
28. Paint houses.
29. Become a gardener.
30. Mow lawns, rake leaves, or shovel snow.

How to Get Started

Now that you have an idea of what side hustles might interest you, it's time to get started. Bringing in your first extra dollar on the side may seem hard, but it's totally doable with a bit of practice and patience. Here are the steps to take to rock your first side hustle.

Step 1: Tell your friends and family.

As the saying goes, it's not what you know, but who you know. The simple act of letting your friends and family know that you are looking to take on extra work can make a world of difference. Your friends and family want to help you, so let them know about your design or writing skills, or that you're available to babysit on weekends. Ask and you shall receive.

Step 2: Mention it on social media.

You may think of side hustling as just something you do on the side, but you're really a small business owner in training. Start by letting others know what you do on your social media profiles, and be sure to use keywords related to your gigs. Make sure people are aware of the services you provide and connect with other influencers and your ideal clientele. Use hashtags appropriately and follow potential clients as well as experts in your field.

Step 3: Create your own platform.

Having your own platform can quickly legitimize your side hustle. Consider starting a blog or creating your own website to advertise your products and services. In today's world, having a piece of digital real estate is key. Imagine if you looked up a restaurant and they didn't have a website. Would you go there? Probably not. The best thing about the internet is that you don't have to be tech savvy to have your own website. You can create a website or blog for free using Weebly or WordPress, or you can choose an inexpensive predesigned website template. I recommend creating a blog in your niche or buying your full name as a domain (i.e. www.melanielockert.com). Make sure that you have a "Work with Me" page as well as a "Contact" page, so it's easy to reach you. You'll want to list all of your products and services—even if you don't feel like an "expert" or have a great deal of experience. Why? Because side hustling is all about gaining experience and trying something new. You're not applying for a salaried job making $100k. What I've learned is that being confident and owning my skills and talents are extremely useful when it comes to landing gigs.

Step 4: Create profiles on various websites.

Depending on your side hustle, you can sign up for relevant websites to help get you hired. Now more than ever, we live in a digitally immersed world with a heavy focus on the sharing economy. There's so many ways to get started making money without having to wait weeks to get paid. Here are some of my favorite sites to help you get started.

- **Writing/Social Media:** CloudPeeps.com, Upwork.com, Contently.com
- **Driving:** Uber.com, Lyft.com

- **Delivery:** Postmates.com, Instacart.com, Seamless.com
- **Pet sitting:** DogVacay.com, Care.com, Rover.com
- **Variety of Gigs:** TaskRabbit.com, Craigslist.org
- **Tutoring:** Tutor.com
- **Brand Ambassador:** EventSpeak.com, Facebook groups —search "Brand Ambassadors of [Your City]"

Even signing up for a handful of these sites can help you find work quickly. There's no need to wait for someone else to create work for you; you can create it yourself!

Step 5: Kick butt and get awesome reviews.

Landing your first side gig may seem tough, but once you get the first one, it gets much easier. Don't let fear get in the way of making money! Rock your side hustle by doing a great job and asking clients for testimonials and reviews. Once you do that, you'll feel more confident and it will be easier to get more gigs.

Side hustling can be addictive and can even help pave a path to a new career. It did for me! After starting my blog, and finally getting a full-time job six months later, I was still side hustling to pay off debt. I thought freelance writing was a great side hustle so I started writing blog posts for twenty-five dollars. My writing career took off and eventually I quit my $31,000 per year nonprofit job and I was able to double my income. Earning more money helped me reach my debt freedom goals even earlier than I expected. That's the beautiful thing about the side hustle: it can be a part-time venture or lead to more if you want it to. It's up to you. You never know where it will lead!

What You Should Know About Side Hustling

For most side hustles, you are going to be an independent contractor, not an employee. This means that you are responsible for paying your own taxes. When I first started side hustling, I thought it was awesome that my income wasn't getting taxed. That was until I was hit with a surprise tax bill. You must report your side hustle income and also pay taxes on it. Your employer is required to send you a 1099 if you made more than $600, but even if you made less than that, you still need to report the income and pay taxes on it. I recommend creating a separate savings account for taxes and deducting at least 20 percent of your income every time you get paid—potentially more, depending on your tax rate. Seek advice from a professional if you're unsure.

As a side hustler, you are essentially running your own business. If you have to buy certain clothes or supplies for your side hustle, or need to drive to an event, you can deduct certain expenses and mileage related to your gig. You should keep your receipts organized using an app like Expensify, which allows you to snap photos of receipts on the go. The key is to stay organized, save money for taxes, and always ask for referrals!

How to Rock the Side Hustle

Through side hustling, you can make a few hundred dollars per month, a few hundred dollars per week, or even more—it's up to you. Once you get your first gig, it will be easier to get the next one. As a side hustler, your reputation and work can make a huge difference. In order to rock the side hustle you'll need to do the following.

- **Show up on time and be polite.** This seems obvious, but you'd be surprised how much this can set you apart. Your reputation is your greatest marketing asset, so be kind and show up on time. It will make you memorable.
- **Give 100 percent.** Whether you're cleaning someone's house, driving them to the airport, or designing a friend's website, give it your all even if you don't love the job or you think it's "below" you. Sometimes you have to take the work that you can get, while reminding yourself of the bigger picture which is *debt freedom.*
- **Follow up.** For every side hustle, send a follow-up email to thank your clients for their time and let them know that you're available in the future. You want to make sure you're top of mind to customers and clients.
- **Try new things.** Side hustling is one of the few times that you can actually experiment and try something new. I've had a lot of fun, enjoyed new experiences, and learned many skills through side hustling.

I truly believe that everybody has the power to earn more money. Everyone has something to offer, and in the sharing economy there are so many ways to monetize your skills and time. The key is to use that extra money wisely by paying off debt, building an emergency fund, and creating a strong financial future. Go get 'em!

Dear Debt,

I'm just not that into you.

Love,
M

CHAPTER 13

———•———

How to Negotiate Your Salary and Boost Your Income

Now you know how to rock the side hustle, but do you know how to earn more money at your day job? Or any future jobs? The secret to making more money at your current or future job is the art of negotiation. The problem is that many of us aren't negotiating—I used to be one of them. After seeing the aftermath of the Great Recession and also dealing with my own high debt and underemployment, I was simply happy to have a job...any job. It's good to be grateful, but negotiating can also set the scale for how much you will earn over your lifetime. Settling for a low salary or choosing not to negotiate can cost you thousands of dollars over the course of your career.

Are You Leaving Money on the Table?

A recent survey by NerdWallet and Looksharp found that only 38 percent of new college graduates negotiated with their employers after receiving an employment offer. That means that more than half of graduates are just accepting the salary offered to them. The real kicker? Out of all of the employers that were surveyed, 76 percent reported that employees who negotiated salaries appeared confident for doing so. Not only that, but three-quarters of employers also said that they had room to negotiate and could increase salaries by 5 to 10 percent. The lesson here is that negotiating can make you appear confident and also increase your salary up to 10 percent right off the bat. Sounds like a win-win situation to me.

The Cost of Not Negotiating

Before you shake your head and dismiss the idea of negotiating your salary, simply thinking that it's too scary or makes you appear greedy, let's look at some examples of what *not negotiating* could cost you. Let's say that you were offered an entry-level job for $30,000 per year. That's a modest salary and depending on where you live, it could be a struggle to meet your basic living expenses (though I've lived in LA on that salary—tough, but doable). If you negotiated a 5 to 10 percent increase you could increase your salary by $1,500 to $3,000 per year. While that might not seem like that much money, over time it adds up.

Using a $3,000 raise, you can:
- Shave months off your student loan repayment
- Build an emergency fund
- Fund a Roth IRA
- Invest it (If you invest $3,000 and don't touch it for forty years, given an 8 percent annual return, you will have $65,173.56.)

This is what's at stake if you don't negotiate your salary. You could build a life of financial security and get eons ahead by negotiating a small increase now.

Why Don't We Negotiate?

As I mentioned, I never negotiated my salary when I had a full-time job. I worked as an employee for nearly a decade and never once asked for more money. Now, I am kicking myself that I lost out on precious money because I didn't ask for more. I only started to master the art of negotiating once I became self-employed, because I had to. Being my own boss forced me to ask for what I'm worth and then always ask for more.

Here's the thing. When an employer is offering you a job, they have already made the mental decision that you are the right candidate. The worst thing they could say is no. It is highly unlikely that they would renege on their job offer. So, really what do you have to lose? If you are a new graduate, or even if you have already been working for a few years, it's crucial that you negotiate and ask for more. You don't know until you ask, and asking is powerful!

How to Negotiate

Now you know the cost of not negotiating and some of the reasons why people avoid it. Most of it comes from fear. It's scary asking for what you are worth. We're scared of being perceived differently or being rejected. But the only way to work through fear is to actually move through it. So, how do you negotiate? Well, it's a multi-step process and one you should start today!

Step 1: Start researching.

The first step in preparing to negotiate is to do your research. Negotiating is a finely crafted skill that requires real numbers to back it up. You can't just negotiate any rate that you want for the job you have. It's important to know what people in your geographic area and your field are earning. For example, a marketing manager in New York City will make a different salary than a marketing manager somewhere in the Midwest. Start by looking at Payscale and Glassdoor to get an idea of salary ranges in your field and geographic area. This will help you to not overshoot your salary or completely undersell yourself. If you have specialized skills and services, then consider going for the top range salary. You want to value yourself and ask for what you are worth! If you know a second language or have unique technical skills, then it's possible you can command more.

Step 2: Practice.

After you've done your research, begin to practice, practice, practice! You'll want to practice your negotiation skills with friends, family, and in the mirror. If you want to go an extra step you can even practice on camera. Practicing helps smooth any rough edges in your approach. It will also help you test what works and what doesn't.

You'll want to practice various scenarios:
- What will you do if they say yes?
- What will you do if they say no?
- How will you react if they want to negotiate and compromise?

During your practice sessions, it's important to know what your minimum acceptable salary is. If they offer you $40,000, but your minimum is $45,000, are you willing to walk away? You don't want to settle for less or you will risk being resentful of a job that you don't really want. You should also know your middle ground and high point for your desired salary. This will allow you to dictate a plan of action depending on your prospective employer's response. It's key to practice and prepare for a variety of situations so that you are not caught off guard.

Step 3: Cultivate your tools and strategies.

In addition to practicing and preparing, you'll want to cultivate a box of tools and resources to help you along with negotiations. Personally, I believe Ramit Sethi is one of the best in the field. His Briefcase Technique has helped land him and many of his students thousands of dollars in raises. The Briefcase Technique can help set you apart from other candidates and showcase your talents. Not only that, it can show why you are truly the best candidate because it shows that you are a problem solver. When your employer is about to offer you a job, open your briefcase and take out a proposal of all your suggestions of how to improve the company. Doing this shows that you have studied up and done your research on the company and that you are forward-thinking and ready to solve problems. Job candidates can often talk too much about themselves, but what employers really want is someone that can solve problems and take things off their plate. How will you make your employer's life easier? How will you add to the company culture and drive the company forward? Answering these questions and illustrating your ideas of how you will improve the company can help you command a higher salary.

Step 4: Know your scripts.

So, you have been offered a job and a starting salary. Whether you like the salary or not, it's time to negotiate. If you are unhappy with the offer, this is a must. But even if you are comfortable with the salary, it doesn't hurt to ask for more. You can start by saying, "I'm so excited about this opportunity and appreciate your offer. Given my skills and abilities, I was hoping for $45,000 for this position. Can we look at a starting salary of $45,000?" It's key to be polite, but also stand your ground. If they say yes, you can reply, "Great, thanks so much for this opportunity. I look forward to growing with the company!" If they say no, will you walk away or negotiate further? You can say, "Is there a number in between that we could settle on?" If there's not a salary that you can agree upon, see if there are any other perks that you can negotiate, such as working from home one day a week, or working an alternative schedule such as four 10-hour days a week, etc.

While it may seem like your employer holds all the cards, remember they are choosing you and they think you are the best fit for their company. It's a two-way street. You are not shooting yourself in the foot by negotiating. Remember, the majority of employers think you appear confident for doing so! So whether you're a new graduate or have been in the workforce for some time, it's crucial that you negotiate. If you don't, you could be leaving thousands of dollars on the table, which ultimately can set you back financially. Using the additional funds, you can pay down debt or use it to invest. Think about it this way: Can you afford to not negotiate?

———•◦•———

Dear Debt,

We've known each other for ten years, and we've been pretty serious for the last five. It's been fun—we've gone to school together, rented our first apartment (which was pretty nice by the way), and picked up a few gadgets and a car or two along the way.

Unfortunately, I don't think we can last. I've given up more time than I can count trying to work with you, to pay you off, and yet you're still here. We've tried to work through our problems, and when I lost my job, you took a little break. But you were right back at it when I got my new job. And don't get me started on that trip to the hospital a few years back. Really, it's kind of a pain to keep you around. You take and take, but it's been a long time since you've given me anything in return.

One day, I know you'll be gone, and I'll be able to live my life and enjoy the freedoms I want to experience. One day, I'll remember you as a distant memory with the ups and downs we had. Mostly downs, really. We still have a ways to go, more years than I'd like to admit. But piece by piece, I'm untangling the way you've woven yourself into my mind, heart, and soul. We've already started to distance ourselves from each other, especially this year when I saved money and worked hard as a tutor to let go of what little control you still had over my credit cards. That was an amazing feeling, and I can't wait to push you out of other parts of my life. Soon, you won't be riding with me every time I go for a drive.

I know we'll probably run into each other every now and then. You might be there for my wedding, when I buy my first home, and maybe my next car or two. But really it's for the best that we don't make it a habit. You go your way, and I'll go mine.

Can't promise you I won't warn all my friends to stay away from you, though. Just saying. It's been real.

Ryan

CHAPTER 14

You Never Know Where a Connection Will Lead

Life can sometimes feel like fractured moments that don't really connect. When you're hustling and paying off debt, it can feel like you are just going from one moment to the next without any time to breathe. It can be tough to look at the bigger picture and realize what you're ultimately working toward. I remember feeling like all of these gigs I worked didn't connect with my ultimate purpose. It was a gig to help me get by and once it was done, it was done. I got paid a little cash and that was it. But over the years, I've learned something important: you never know where something will lead. After seeing opportunities come from unlikely places, I now believe this as one of the core tenets of my business, and I try to treat every opportunity and connection equally.

A Connection is an Opportunity

When I was struggling looking for a job, I did everything I thought I was supposed to. I wrote unique cover letters and updated my resume for each job. I researched the company and consumed a lot of content on how to rock interviews. If you've struggled to find work, you know how disheartening it is to not hear back after you've submitted an application. At least if you get an interview you know you did something right, but when you don't hear a peep, it can feel isolating and lonely.

When I first started my blog, I couldn't find a full-time job for the life of me. I tried all the traditional avenues. I applied relentlessly and kept sending shot after shot in the dark, hoping someone would give me a chance and realize that I wasn't some sort of loser. For so long, I was only looking to do things the traditional way because that's all I knew. But once I started side hustling and trying new things, more opportunities came my way.

I now know that the best things in life rarely come from constructed opportunities or scripted events. They just happen, in an unlikely place, at an unlikely time. Through changing my approach and being open to new experiences and opportunities, I've been able to pave a new path for myself. I created a job for myself, doing something that I love and helping others. Now I work as a full-time writer and event planner and help others get out of debt. As my friend once told me, I've turned my pain into my passion. All of these opportunities came about as the result of the platform I created and the connections I built.

I used to think that a blog was just a diary, but really it can be so much more. You can leverage it to brand your voice and build a community. You can get jobs you didn't even know existed and create opportunities for yourself without even sending out a resume. Here's a glimpse into some of the ways that my connections have turned into opportunities.

Networking In Person

Before I started my blog, I reached out to a fellow blogger in Portland. I didn't know the first thing about blogging, but I knew that I had to shift my negative emotions related to debt into something positive. Without meeting her and receiving her encouragement, I may have never started my blog. Through her, I met other bloggers, most of whom helped launch my freelance writing career. Their support helped me get experience and showcase my writing chops.

Social Media

One of the main ways I've been able to get new gigs and opportunities is through social media. Social media doesn't have to be only about vacation pics, cat videos, and baby photos. It can be a lucrative networking tool when used properly. I met one of my business partners on Twitter, when we connected over the fact that she lives in Brooklyn, where I used to live. I dug her work and got in touch. That simple connection has now launched a different aspect of my business. One of my other writing clients saw that I enjoy Twitter and asked me to manage their social media, to which I happily obliged and got an increase in pay. I also got a consultant gig from a company that I followed on Twitter when I sent a simple message that said, "I love your mission!" A relationship formed and now we are great colleagues. In addition to Twitter, I found one of my best paying clients through a Facebook group. There are Facebook groups for nearly everything, so join groups in your field and start networking!

Sending Cold Pitches

Aside from using social media to get gigs, I've also sent cold pitches to companies, offering my services. I pitched a company in my niche and said that I loved their content, but that there was just one problem: there were no female voices. I boldly sent an email and said I'd love to add my voice to the mix. Now I'm a writer for their site.

Last year at the Financial Bloggers Conference (FinCon), I met someone for approximately ten seconds. I was on my way out the door, but we both joked that we should "network" and exchange business cards. We did, and I didn't give it much thought. After FinCon, I spent hours sending every person that I met a unique follow-up email, and my ten-second connection turned into one of my largest partnerships.

As a blogger, I receive a lot of press releases. Many bloggers tend to delete these as trash or unwanted spam, but in most cases I respond if I think my services would be a good fit. I once responded and pitched an idea for an event after receiving a press release from a company. This response led to a deeper connection and resulted in a powerful event with a national brand.

Trying a Different Approach

So often we think that we are doing things the "right way," but our methods are clearly not working. Try to step outside of yourself and see what you could be doing differently. Your approach is everything; I cannot emphasize that enough. If your current approach is not working, stop beating a dead horse. Try something new. Be bold, ask for what you want, and be confident in what you can deliver.

We all have to deal with the perils of Impostor Syndrome coming to rain down on our parade, but get an umbrella and keep going. You never know where a connection will lead. You never know where your next gig will come from. Opportunities are right around the corner. The key is to keep at it and put yourself out there, everywhere. Be unabashedly yourself.

If you're looking to start a business, get a new job, fall in love, whatever it may be, and what you're doing isn't working, try something new. Keep putting yourself out there on social media and follow up with everyone you meet. Everyone. Your network is your net worth, so foster your connections. Be yourself and believe there is something out there for you that is greater than yourself.

———— •◦• ————

Dear Debt,

We've known each other a long time now. I suppose we kind of grew up together in a way. We first met when I was eighteen and had just moved across the country to go to college. I was young and naïve, and it was fine because we were really just casual friends. But when I was twenty and went to law school I ended up seeing a lot more of you. Truth be told, I didn't realize then just how much of you I would see or how long our relationship would last. For years I went about life just assuming I'd always be stuck with you in my life, the guest from the party that just never leaves. However, living without a roommate this past summer forced me to take a good hard look at my finances, and I realized just how much you were costing me. I thought back to when I was in high school and my plan had been to meet up with you in school, spend my twenties living on the cheap and paying you off by the time I was thirty.

Granted, I could not have predicted the recession and how it affected my job prospects, but looking at things now, I'm no longer willing to just let you hang around forever. So from now on I'm going to keep you close. You know what they say, keep your friends close and your enemies closer. Guess what, Debt—I just became your best frenemy. I'll walk next to you for a good long while still, I'll eat lunch with you and remember to wear pink on Wednesdays, but all the while I'll be doing everything I can to bring you down. I'll be making frequent extra payments, cutting you down one loan at a time, until you are no longer relevant in my life. Because honestly Debt, you'd be nothing if it wasn't for your high interest rates on high balances and my poor decisions. Well I'm making better decisions now and they are going to impact the other things you've got going on. You are going down.

XOXO,
Your Best Frenemy

This letter was written by Liz.

PART 4

Lessons from Paying
Off Debt

CHAPTER 15

The Secret to Getting Out of Debt

On December 10th, 2015, I made my very last student loan payment. I kept logging into my loan servicer's account, eagerly waiting for it to show my updated balance. On the afternoon of December 11th, I logged in and saw this:

$ Current Balance:	$0.00 >
📅 Due Date:	N/A

As I saw the number zero before me, a wave of emotion hit me. My breathing got shorter and my eyes started to tear up. All of the years spent working odd jobs, working nights, weekends, and holidays, and cutting my budget back to the bone finally paid off. I had been waiting for this day my whole life. Instantly, I felt a huge weight lifted off of my shoulders. For the very first time in my adult life, I was debt free.

My journey out of debt included a lot of twists and turns, setbacks and successes. I could have never imagined the path that laid ahead. While I've been paying off debt since 2007, I didn't get serious about it until I graduated from NYU in May 2011. After a long period of depression and underemployment, I started my blog in January 2013 to keep me accountable for paying off my debt. In the early days of my blog, I felt hopeless. The life I had hoped I would have after graduation didn't pan out. I didn't have a fabulous career, living in New York, taking advantage of all that life had to offer. Instead, I moved to Portland to be with my partner and save money. While my relationship was strong, I felt defeated by everything else. I couldn't find a job, I had very few interviews, and I felt like there was an elephant the size of my debt sitting on my chest. In those days, every day felt like a struggle. I had to go on food stamps to get by. I was embarrassed and sad with how things had ended up, and I internalized it as all being my fault, like I wasn't good enough, like I deserved it. It wasn't until I made a commitment to get out of debt—regardless of my circumstances—that everything changed. Instead of just letting things happen to me and waiting for opportunities, I worked my ass off to make things happen.

In a weird way, I have to thank my debt. I've learned so much about the power of hard work, sacrifice, and believing in myself. I've pushed myself to my limits and learned new skills. Throughout the years of writing about my experience with debt, I started writing about personal finance for a living, leading up to this book that you are reading. I now realize that everything in my debt-free journey is interconnected.

Many people ask me how I got out of debt and want to know the steps I took. I did a lot of things to get out of debt which I've highlighted in this book, including:

- Moving to a location with a lower cost of living

- Cutting back on unnecessary expenses
- Earning more (this was a big one for me) through side hustling and freelancing
- Paying off high interest debt first (the debt avalanche method)
- Making multiple payments throughout the month to lower the amount of interest that was accruing daily

But the biggest thing I did to get out of debt? I changed my mindset. From a financial standpoint, paying off debt is as simple as spending less and earning more. In fact, most personal finance problems can be solved in the same way. To pay off debt, you need to make more money, spend less, and put more toward debt. But if that's the answer, why do so many of us struggle to get out of debt? Why do so many of us struggle to build wealth? It's our mindset. Think about the way you were raised and how money affected your upbringing. Think about certain cultural or societal assumptions you may carry that affect the way you view money.

I grew up in a modest family—not rich, not poor—but throughout my life, my dad was often without a job. I never felt that we had a lot of money. My parents had working class upbringings and grew up with much less than I had. I grew up with the belief that money was evil and that people who wanted money were greedy. As a young adult, I bought what everyone was telling me and unabashedly believed that student loans were "good debt." Not only that, but as a creative person majoring in the arts, I thought that I'd never make a lot of money and that I was destined to live a life of struggle and poverty—that it was my choice, and that it was a noble choice. But I was wrong. I now see how my long-held beliefs about money affected my money mindset as well as my spending triggers.

Deciding to get out of debt once and for all required me to shift my mindset in a lot of ways. I could no longer hide behind the idea that I was going to be in debt forever. Instead, I had to look at the numbers and question every expense. I had to let go of a lot of things I thought I deserved. One of the biggest shifts I had to make was letting go of what I thought my life would look like. I was in my late twenties and early thirties when I was busting my butt to get out of debt. Many of my friends were getting married, buying houses, and doing things that people my age are supposed to do. During my quest to be debt free, I let go of all the things I thought my life would be—having a successful career and a nice home and traveling a lot—and focused on paying off debt instead. Because of this, I did some jobs that previously I would have shunned. I ignored any of the things I thought I "should" do at my age and continued to live like a broke college student in a lot of ways. During this time, I had to learn to be strong about getting out of debt, especially in social situations.

Our peers and society have a whole lot of influence on us, whether we want to believe so or not. Now with social media, we have another way to observe the metaphorical Joneses. We scroll through Facebook and Instagram looking at everyone's beautiful photos of exotic vacations, their latest adventures, or their newest clothing purchases. Everyone's life looks so perfect on social media. In reality, it's a curated highlight reel of only the best stuff—we don't see the hard times, the credit card bills, the blood, sweat, and tears. If you're working to get out of debt, you may want to take a social media hiatus and ignore all the messages in your feed that could inadvertently encourage you to spend more. Though I think social media can be a powerful tool for building community and getting side hustles, for the most part it can negatively affect our money mindset. Your mindset is the toughest thing to change and the key ingredient to getting out of debt.

In order to change your mindset to get out of debt, you need to let go of things like:

- Thinking "I deserve this..."
- Thinking "I need this..." (when you really don't)
- Thinking you'll pay it off "later"
- Waiting for your family, partner, friend, or government to help you out of your situation
- Thinking that "everyone is in debt," so it's not that bad
- Thinking of student loans as "good debt"
- Believing that nice things will make you feel good, happy, and successful
- Practicing expensive habits that don't serve your bottom line

Change is hard. You've been conditioned your whole life to believe certain things about money, life, and work. Committing to getting out of debt means rejecting the status quo. Let's face it, many Americans are up to their eyeballs in debt. Between student loan payments, a car note, mortgage payments, and a credit card balance—debt is the norm. In other words, you have to go against the current in order to get out of debt and not live in the status quo. It's tough and challenging and can put a strain on your relationships, but it's key to remember your "why." What is the ultimate reason why you want to get out of debt?

How to Change Your Money Mindset

Changing your money mindset is a process that won't happen overnight. You have to put in the time and hard work to let change take over. When you first commit to paying off debt and changing your money mindset, it's likely you will struggle. You'll want to go back to the way things were, thinking and doing things the way you always have. Our comfort zone is just that: comfortable. But progress happens when we get out of our comfort zone. Luckily, there are a few key things you can do to shift your money mindset into something that will help you pay off debt and attract financial success in your life.

Tip #1: Practice gratitude.

When I was broke and struggling, feeling overwhelmed with my debt and thinking it would never go away, I was depressed by everything that I didn't have. I was so low that I ended up in therapy (which I found on the cheap at the local graduate counseling school), because in reality I was a hot mess. My therapist suggested that every day I write down three things that I was grateful for. It could be anything from the hot coffee I had, to a nice walk, or even a nap. At first, I thought this was new-age crap and I rolled my eyes, but like a good student I tried it out. An amazing thing happened when I took five minutes out of my day to write down, with pen and paper, three things that I was grateful for. Doing this exercise made me realize that even without a lucrative career and having so much debt, I was wealthier than most in the world. I had a roof over my head, food on the table, love, and family. By focusing my mental energy on being grateful for what I had, rather than being depressed by what I didn't have, I slowly started to shift my money mindset. Once I felt the deep gratitude of what I already had, the pull of buying new things lessened.

Tip #2: Turn jealousy into productivity.

Jealousy, the green-eyed monster, is a pervasive and intricate emotion that can have a major impact on our life and success. It can get under our skin and make us doubt the very core of our being. It can turn us into mean, ugly people and can lead us to spend more money trying to play catch up. Maybe it's a certain lifestyle, income, career, or skill that you wish you had. If you find yourself feeling jealous, first think about why it is that you're jealous. What do others have that you want? Write it down. Jealousy can cost you money if you try to keep up with others, and it can keep you stagnant and immobile. Instead of letting the green-eyed monster take over, ask yourself what steps you can take to improve your situation. Realize that someone you may be jealous of once started where you are, so you can't compare your beginning to someone else's middle. If he or she accomplished something or has something that you want, let that inspire you instead of consuming you with jealousy.

I used to be consumed by jealousy and would waste time festering in my feelings. Now, I realize how much time I wasted comparing myself to others and being jealous. Imagine how much you can improve yourself and your situation if you work on yourself and your goals instead of focusing on others. Instead of being jealous, let the people you are jealous of inspire you to take action. Ask them to be your mentor. Connect with them. I've realized an important lesson over the years. Instead of wanting to be the best, you should strive to have a network that is more successful than you. You should not be the smartest person in the room. When you connect and build relationships with others that have achieved what you want, you can learn great lessons from them. So the next time you're feeling the pang of jealousy, ask yourself what steps you can take to get closer to attaining what you want. That's how you can turn jealousy into productivity.

Tip #3: Choose delayed gratification.

When you're getting out of debt, you need to question every single expense. Ask yourself, "Do I actually need this? Will it make my life better or easier?" Asking these questions can help you choose delayed gratification. Delaying gratification can help shift your money mindset from toxic behaviors that we have normalized over the course of our lives. Oftentimes we get in a routine of doing things a certain way that could potentially be detrimental to our budget.

The first step that you need to take is to ween yourself off of ingrained habits. If you're used to going to Starbucks or buying your lunch every day, it's going to be tough to change when that's what you're used to. Start by cutting down to three times a week, then once a week. Start replacing your old habits with new ones, like making coffee at home or packing your lunch.

Choosing delayed gratification can improve your impulse control and help you make better choices with your money, which is key when paying off debt. I know how intense the feeling can be when you really want something *now*. Give it forty-eight hours. Once you delay gratification and give yourself some perspective, the power of that purchase won't be as strong, and you may realize that you don't even want it anymore. When you practice delayed gratification and actually save money by not making a purchase, put that extra money that would have been spent toward debt!

Tip #4: Believe you are a money-making machine.

Your money mindset is the foundation for everything that you believe about money. It affects your relationship with money, spending, earnings, and much more. For so long, I operated from a place of scarcity. I thought there weren't enough jobs or money to go around and that I'd never have enough. I was jealous, petty, and constantly worried. Once I started to side hustle, my confidence started to grow. I realized just how many ways I could monetize my time and skills. I started to look at things differently and see how much opportunity and abundance is out there. I realized that just because one person was wealthy and successful, it didn't mean that I couldn't be as well. Instead of constantly telling myself that I was broke, I started to tell myself that I was a money-making machine. I started believing that work and money-making opportunities were everywhere. Once I started to see things differently and looked at everything as an opportunity rather than a setback, I started earning a lot more money. One way that you can practice this belief is by saying, "I'm a money-making machine" in the shower or while looking in the mirror. Sounds cheesy, I know, but it can put you in a position to attract money and financial success.

Tip #5: Believe that challenges are opportunities.

When times are tough, it's easy to get consumed with how hard everything is, and you may want to give up. Debt repayment can often feel like a heavy burden on your shoulders, sucking the soul and energy out of you. But there's a way that you can shift your mindset from one of struggle to one of abundance. Instead of thinking of all the hard times as challenges that you simply have to go through, think of them as opportunities to learn something new.

When I was struggling to find work, pay off debt, and find my place in the world, everything felt hard and many days I found myself in tears wondering what my purpose was. I couldn't find any direction. It's hard to learn from our hard times when we're going through them. We're focused on getting through them and surviving, not thinking of any of the lessons hidden beneath the surface. Eventually I realized that I didn't have the confines of a nine-to-five job or any major responsibilities. Instead of focusing on the challenge, I started focusing on the opportunity. It was at that point that I came up with the idea for my blog and began writing. Shifting my energy into something positive and thinking of the opportunities that I could create from my hard times helped me stay afloat.

Lessons Learned from Paying Off Debt

I'm not going to lie. Getting out of debt was the hardest thing I've ever had to do. It made me question a lot of things and put me through the wringer, but now I'm grateful for the experience. Paying off debt taught me so many priceless lessons about life and myself that I may not have learned otherwise. If you're in the thick of debt repayment right now and thinking how bad it feels, look for the silver lining. Here are a few things that debt has taught me.

- **How to live on less.** In today's commercialized world, it's easy to get caught up in getting the *next big thing* and keeping up with the Joneses. Unfortunately, living that life will keep you in debt. Getting out of debt forced me to live on less and focus on what really matters: health, love, and happiness. Those things don't have to cost any money either!
- **The power of a dollar.** Before paying off debt, I had never really focused on how much things cost, how much I made, how much interest I was paying, etc. In other words, I was absolutely oblivious. When I committed to paying off debt, I started to actually pay attention to the power of a dollar—how much I was earning after taxes, how far my dollar could take me, how much things cost based on my salary (for example, a lunch out cost me thirty minutes of work). Through paying off debt, I truly learned the power of a dollar.
- **The value of hard work.** I'm the first to admit that I don't think I would have worked this hard if I wasn't in debt. Being in debt put a fire beneath me and compelled me to go above and beyond the obligations of a regular job. I knew that I'd have to be extraordinary and work incredibly hard to get out of debt. I pushed myself out of my comfort zone and did things that I never thought I'd do. Working so hard pushed my boundaries, forced me to learn new things, and taught me a lot about perseverance.

- **The satisfaction of reaching a huge goal.** I had never before set such a huge goal for myself that seemed so insurmountable. Before deciding to pay off my debt, I had stayed put in the confines of my comfort zone. Setting a larger-than-life goal pushed me in so many ways and gave me the confidence I needed to be my own boss and pursue self-employment.

I know that I wouldn't be where I am today without learning these lessons!

Dear Debt,

It's been so long since we last spoke. We've been on quite a journey, huh? We met as teenagers at the ripe old age of seventeen. You were so alluring with your promises, telling me all my dreams would come true. I never doubted you, not even once. But then troubled times hit. You started to drain me emotionally and financially. I lost myself in you and didn't know who I was without you. As much as I tried to fight it, you consumed every fiber of my being.

I was tired of fighting. I was tired of being defined by you. I wanted to take back me. So I started talking about you to all of my friends. I started writing about your conniving ways. I shared my struggles, my dreams, and my hopes of overcoming you with the world. By opening myself up to others and not living in the persecution of my head, or in the shadow of your image, I started to connect with others. I believed I was more than my debt and that I could overcome you. That even as dysfunctional as our relationship is, I could become my own person and remedy the mistakes left in your wake. And from this, I've built a community of people all working against you—a group of friends, mentors, and confidantes that inspire me to do better. Somehow, I've even created a career that was born out of struggle.

My pain became my passion. And herein lies the silver lining. I've found a new path. You haven't changed, but my relationship with you has changed. You no longer have absolute power over me. I've taken back my life and I'm happier than ever.

So while I still hate you and everything you represent, I have to thank you for making me stronger, making me work harder, and giving me a different path in life.

Best,
Melanie

CHAPTER 16

What to Do After You Pay Off Debt

The moment I paid off my debt was an odd one. I had fantasized about the moment for so many years, but when it actually happened, I surprised myself. I saw the balance at zero and my chest tightened and I started hyperventilating. I couldn't believe it. The reality felt overwhelming. I started to tear up, remembering every moment that I wanted to give up. I thought about all of the good, bad, and ugly side hustles, and everything I went through. After about twenty minutes I started jumping, screaming, and dancing around my living room like a crazy person. I thought the day would never come, but here it was.

I've only been debt free a few months, but I've realized how important it is to come up with a financial plan after paying off debt. If you don't have a plan, you're likely to feel a bit lost and confused about what to do next. Paying off debt is such a huge accomplishment and can take up all of your energy. Without debt, it's easy to succumb to lifestyle inflation and move forward without an action plan for your money. I was putting up to four thousand dollars per month toward debt—not an insignificant amount. Now that I'm debt free, I'm committed to using those funds to build an emergency fund, catch up on retirement savings, and start investing aggressively. I'm ready to start funding my future, instead of paying for my past.

You may feel like you're never going to get out of debt, but with hard work and perseverance, you will get there. It's important to come up with a financial plan for your money before you're debt free. I've heard from so many people that they felt lost and directionless after paying off debt. They aren't sure what to do next. Getting out of debt is an obvious goal, but what else should you do with your money? Here are some steps that you can take to build a financial plan.

Step 1: Build a fully funded emergency fund.

Emergencies are an inevitable part of life and can come in many shapes and sizes. You could lose your job, get ill, have a car accident, need a home repair, or stumble upon some other unforeseen expense. It's not a matter of if these things happen, but when they will happen. In order to build financial security, it's best to save at least six to twelve months' worth of expenses, should anything happen.

I've experienced bouts of underemployment where I wasn't making enough to survive. I've also been hit with an unexpected hospital visit when I was uninsured, and had a not-so-fun car accident that cost me nearly two thousand dollars in repairs. My emergency fund has saved my butt in times of need. It's prevented me from going further into debt and helped me stay afloat during difficult times. An emergency fund can turn the unexpected into an inconvenience, rather than a crisis. Build up your emergency fund in a separate savings account so that it's not easily accessible, and commit to only touching those funds during real emergencies.

Step 2: Check your credit score and credit report.

Your credit can influence so much of your life. Your credit score, which is a three-digit number representing your creditworthiness, can determine if you get approved for an apartment, credit card, car loan, etc. Your credit report is a comprehensive report that illustrates how much you have borrowed, when the accounts were opened, if you've made late payments, and so on. It's important to check both your credit score and credit report annually.

Once you pay off debt, your credit mix will change and your credit score may go down slightly. That's what happened to me. When I paid off my student loans, I thought that my credit would have a metaphorical party and my credit score would magically increase. But to my surprise, my credit score dropped a few points. I was dismayed, so I decided to look into it. A debtor's credit mix affects his or her credit score, and because I paid off my student loans, I no longer had any installment loans in my credit portfolio. Not only that, but it was my oldest account and it was now closed. Don't let this worry you though! Paying off debt is obviously the best choice. In my case, the drop was only a few points.

Start by checking your credit score and credit report and making sure that it shows your loans are paid off. In addition, it's key to make sure there are no errors, especially before you apply for any type of loan that may involve checking your credit. You can get your free credit score using a service like Credit Karma, and you can access your free credit report once per year through AnnualCreditReport.com. AnnualCreditReport.com works with the three credit bureaus—Experian, TransUnion, and Equifax—to provide you with a free credit report. If you find any errors, be sure to contact the credit bureaus to remedy the mistakes.

Once you've checked your credit score and credit report, work on keeping your credit in good shape by always making on-time payments and keeping your outstanding balances low. Strive to use only 20 to 30 percent of your credit limit. Your credit utilization, which is how much of your established credit limit you are actually using, affects your credit score. So even if you are paying your balances in full each month, if you are charging your cards to the max, you may appear as a risky borrower to your lenders.

Step 3: Max out your 401(k).

If you have a full-time job that offers a 401(k) match, be sure to contribute at least enough to receive the matching contribution from your employer. Essentially, it's free money and a perk of the job, so it behooves you to take advantage of it. As an added bonus, your contributions are deducted from your paycheck on a pre-tax basis.

Even though none of the nonprofits that I worked for offered 401(k) matches, one of my biggest financial regrets is not saving for retirement earlier. I made every excuse in the book. I didn't make enough money. There was no match, so what was the point? I had student loan debt, so why would I focus on retirement? I could save for it later.

Now I'm 31-years-old with nearly nothing saved. I'm catching up for lost time, but if you have a retirement match or access to a 401(k), strive to max it out.

If you don't have a 401(k), consider contributing to a Roth IRA, which is a great investment vehicle for retirement. Your contributions are made with after-tax dollars, which means that when you withdraw funds at retirement age you won't pay any taxes. There are certain income limits to contribute to a Roth IRA, but if you are within the guidelines, it can be a beneficial way to save.

Step 4: Start investing.

Let's face it, for many Millennials, investing can seem foreign or just downright scary. I know that I've often felt that way. Investing can be full of jargon and acronyms that are tough to understand, but as I've come to learn, you shouldn't wait to invest just because you don't understand something. Start getting familiar with the terminology. Read *The Wall Street Journal*. Listen to my friend Shannon's "Martinis and Your Money" podcast where she breaks down investing in a way that's easy to understand. The key is to empower yourself with knowledge so that you have a basis of understanding.

Investing doesn't have to be difficult. The good news is that investing is becoming easier and more accessible thanks to so-called robo-advisors. Robo-advisors typically are online investment firms that automate your investments to maximize returns and minimize losses. For some robo-advisors, you don't need a minimum amount to start investing. These services, like Betterment and Wealthfront, can help you start investing with very little capital for a low monthly fee. You could also learn how to invest on your own with a brokerage account through Fidelity or Vanguard. Just be aware of how much you may be paying in fees. They may seem small, but over the course of thirty or forty years, fees can take a big bite out of your nest egg.

Step 5: Consider short, medium, and long-term goals.

Once you've said your last goodbye to debt, it's time to focus on other important financial goals. It's crucial to list your short, medium, and long-term goals so that you can put your money to work for you. Money is a tool to live a happier life, so allocating your funds that would have otherwise gone toward debt is important. Consider what you want in the next one to five years, five to ten years, and beyond. Some of these items may include things like a trip abroad, raising a child, a down payment on a house, or a new car. Don't hold anything back, and be realistic with what's important to you. In order to get your money to work for you, you need to plan and create a financial plan based on your goals. If you don't write down your goals, it can be harder to save because it will feel like a chore. Listing your goals and being clear about what you need to do in order to reach those goals will help you stay on track and live a purpose-filled life.

When you're debt free, the world really is your oyster and each dollar you earn is yours to keep. Why not build wealth and save for the things that you want? Being rich isn't so much about being a millionaire or reaching a certain status; it's about reaching your goals and being happy and healthy without money getting in the way. Rather, money should be used as a tool to help you get there.

Four Things You Should Invest in to Build a Rich Life

Investing is a key aspect to building wealth for your future. But did you know that there are other things you should invest in besides the stock market? Though money is important, life isn't only about money and you should invest in other areas of your life as well. Here are four things that you should invest in to build a rich, fabulous life.

1. Invest in your health.

Your health is such an important factor in your well-being. As a young person, it can be easy to take your health for granted. However, eating poorly and being indolent now can have serious ramifications down the line. Aside from physical health, your mental health is also important. Stress kills, and depression and anxiety can affect your ability to enjoy life.

Invest in your well-being by eating well and being more physically active—even if it costs more money. This could mean joining a gym, buying running gear, biking, or even getting massages. *Fun fact: Massages can help boost your immunity.*

I read a quote a while back that really resonated with me. It said, "If you don't take care of your body, where will you live?" It reminded me that we have one body and one mind, so it's important to treat it well. As a young person, I sometimes take for granted taking care of myself. But if I don't take care of myself first, then I can't be 100 percent in the other aspects of my life.

2. Invest in people.

Relationships are your most valuable assets in life. Your family, your partner, and your friends are all people that will be there when times get tough (and they do). If you only focus on yourself, you'll start to lose these precious people. Your relationships are what get you through the tough times and help you thrive during the good times. I would be nowhere without my personal network, friends, family, and my partner. I try to show gratitude and give back to them when I can. I love to spend time with them and learn from them. Invest in others and they will return the favor. Support others, and remember, it's not all about you. People are what make life rich, so open yourself up to others and learn something from them.

3. Invest in yourself.

While investing in others is key to maintaining your network, it's also vitally important that you invest in yourself. This means that you should be spending time cultivating your own creativity and ideas, giving yourself permission to succeed and fail, and doing what you want.

I can't speak for all women, but I know there is a lot of pressure to care for everyone but ourselves. We're caregivers at heart and we want to care for our partners, our children, our family, and our co-workers. I am the first to admit that "me time" used to come last. However, I burnt out quickly and felt anxious, depressed, and fatigued. Now I'm practicing self-care, resting, and investing in my own health, happiness, and career.

You have to be your own biggest cheerleader and give yourself permission to be happy and invest in yourself.

That could mean taking a class, a workshop, or even declining work in order to recharge your batteries.

4. Invest in experiences.

Lastly, invest in *experiences* over *things*. Things can weigh you down and clutter your life if you're not careful, but experiences can change your life. My favorite experiences have been traveling, going to see concerts, or eating amazing meals that I could never make myself. Over the years, I've traveled to numerous countries, seen musical greats like Ray Charles and B.B. King, and eaten culinary delights that rocked my world. I enjoy doing things that enhance my vault of experiences and teach me something new. I personally believe that travel changes you each and every time. It reminds you of this much bigger world we live in—and also reminds you of the beauty of home. The value of experiences, while ultimately unquantifiable, will make you much richer.

———————— • ————————

Dear Debt,

I've been meaning to write this letter for a while, but I couldn't find the words. After six years of cursing your name all over town and letting everyone know how much I hated you, I wanted to let you in on a secret: I don't actually hate you. I hate my relationship with you, but I don't hate you. I've spent so much time focusing on how you have brought me down that I've neglected to see the good that you brought me. You have given me an education full of life-changing experiences, critical thinking skills, New York, the drive to pursue my passion, and the clarity to pursue my dreams. You have also hindered some of those very dreams, but overall you propelled me to pursue a lot of my life goals. I got to cross so many off the list because of you.

After years of being on an emotional roller-coaster with you, I want to thank you. I want to thank you for teaching me the value of hard work. Ever since we got together, I knew I had to hustle to make it work between us. I couldn't rest on my laurels hoping everything would work out. I had to take action. I needed to show myself that I could pursue my dreams and be the woman I was meant to be. You gave me a path and taught me a few tricks along the way.

Without you, I would have never been so inspired to try new things, explore possibilities, and engage with people in new ways. Before you, complacency and comfort were my destiny. I stayed in my comfort zone, isolating myself from the bigger picture. Since we've met, I've been so inspired and motivated to be the best version of myself.

I used to see myself as better than certain jobs and more successful than others. I've been completely humbled by you. I've learned to let go of my ego and think about our partnership. I rolled up my sleeves and got my hands dirty cleaning up after wealthier people, cleaning toilets, picking up trash, and taking care of someone else's kid. I am now more empathetic to those silent pioneers that are holding up the world, doing the invisible, but very important dirty work. I'm connected to the working class because I am working to make a better life for us.

As you know, it hasn't always been easy. I've resented what you have done to me and I wanted to give up completely. The adjustment and learning curve proved to be too much. But at the end of the day, you were my turning point. I moved from thought to action. I've pursued dreams and here I am writing about our relationship for all the world to see. You have made me a better person, and for that I thank you. I want to thank you for making me who I am today: a fighter, a worker, a dreamer, a go-getter, and an inspired writer. I couldn't have done it without you.

Love,
Melanie

CHAPTER 17

How Paying Off Debt Changed My Life—and Can Change Yours Too

When I first started getting serious about debt repayment, the journey felt so long. I was beginning on a path with a million miles ahead of me. There were moments of exhaustion, fatigue, frustration, and wanting to give up. There were also moments of excitement, like getting my debt under $50,000, paying off my 7.9 percent loans, and making my first $3,000 payment. I dreamed of being debt free for so long, but I couldn't imagine what it felt like. After all, I was in debt for all of my adult life. Now, I've been debt free for a few months and I couldn't be happier. My money is now 100 percent mine. I am rebuilding my savings and will start aggressively investing.

For years, I felt I could never truly relax, knowing that I owed money. I never felt like my money was *truly mine*, because it wasn't. Every purchase caused a pang of anxiety. Each month I'd nervously calculate how much I could afford to put toward debt. After each payment, I'd see how much was going toward interest and would feel defeated for a moment. Every payment felt like moving two steps forward and one step back.

It was a tough journey that lasted nine years, but now that I am living debt free, it's a whole new world. I feel rich. Aside from keeping more of my money, I feel like I have more freedom and choices. I'm self-employed. When I was in debt, I felt like I had to take every gig that came my way. How could I say no to money? But now that I'm debt free, I can afford to be pickier. When the cards are in your hands and you can take on work for reasons aside from just money, you have the power. It feels damn good. I can afford to be spontaneous. Over the holidays, I went to the coast for some relaxation. We were having such a good time that we decided to stay another night on a whim. While I was paying off debt, I would have never done that.

Getting out of debt changed my life and gave me the freedom to live, no longer shackled by its chains. It's given me happiness, freedom, and spontaneity. Not only that, but getting out of debt has taught me so many priceless life lessons.

There are many factors that make it difficult to get out of debt including the rising cost of living, stagnant wages, and a lackluster economy. There are many things outside of our control that can affect our success. I acknowledge that, and also the privilege that many of us have. However, I do think the narrative surrounding debt needs to change. It is possible to get out of debt, and it's not something that we should all just accept as part of the status quo. As long as you're in debt, you're a prisoner. Fighting to get out of debt is fighting for your freedom.

Now that I'm on the other side, I want to help others believe they can do it too. Will it be easy? No. Will it be worth it? You bet. I know you can do it. What are your debt-free dreams?

----●●----

Dear Debt,

I thought you were the end of me, but it was really just the beginning. It's been five years since I left and things have changed so much. My money is mine to keep. Without you, I've grown my net worth, emergency fund, and retirement accounts. I work freelance on a variety of creative projects. I travel several times a year and volunteer for causes I'm passionate about. My life is in focus and I am in the driver's seat. I can make decisions without thinking about you. I have the freedom to relentlessly pursue my dreams and create the best version of myself.

I was never happy with you. You were a terrible lover and an even worse friend. You distorted my vision of who I am, my self-worth, and what I could become. I'm glad I kicked your ass to the curb when I did. I now see how courageous I was to face you, in light of all the obstacles. I heard you've been around the block, spreading lies and spewing bullshit, selling women your idea of a better life. I can see through you; you're just a desperate leech looking for attention.

I've hated you for so long and resented everything about you, but I thank you for making me stronger. Thank you for showing me what I don't want. I've moved on and I've forgiven you. And I'm finally free.

Sincerely,
M

APPENDIX

Dear Debt Worksheets

When I think of money, I…

_____

_____

_____

_____

Money makes me feel…

_____

_____

_____

_____

How would making $100 more per month change your life?

_____

_____

_____

_____

_____

_____

How would making $500 more per month change your life?

_____

_____

_____

_____

_____

_____

How would making $1,000 more per month change your life?

_____

_____

_____

_____

_____

_____

My dream salary is _____

What assumptions about money are holding you back?

_____

_____

_____

_____

_____

_____

_____

What kind of debt do you have? (loans, credit cards, etc.)

_____

_____

_____

_____

_____

_____

How much do you owe?

Debt #1: _____

Debt #2: _____

Debt #3: _____

Debt #4: _____

What are the interest rates on your loans?

Debt #1: _____

Debt #2: _____

Debt #3: _____

Debt #4: _____

Which debt payoff method will you choose, debt avalanche or debt snowball?

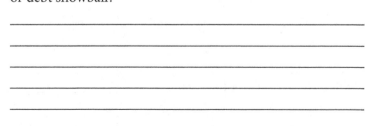

Which side hustles can help you pay off debt?

_____

_____

_____

_____

_____

_____

What will your life after debt look like?

_____

_____

_____

_____

_____

_____

What inspires you to get out of debt?

_____

_____

_____

_____

_____

_____

I will be debt free (Month, Year): _____

ACKNOWLEDGEMENTS

This book would not be possible without the help of many people. Thank you to my readers for following my journey and continuing to inspire me every day. Thank you to my family and my partner for always rooting for me, even when I wanted to give up. Thank you to all the Dear Debt letter authors who've been brave enough to share their stories. Thank you to everyone who has given me a voice and allowed me to make writing my career. Thank you to all of the friends I've met through blogging, for encouraging me and inspiring me along the way.

A portion of this book originally appeared in my posts for the following sites:
- The College Investor: TheCollegeInvestor.com
- Money Ning: MoneyNing.com
- Dear Debt: DearDebt.com

Thank you to the following Dear Debt letter authors for allowing their letters to be published in this book:
- Steven from Even Steven Money. Visit Steven's website at EvenStevenMoney.com.
- Latoya from Life and a Budget. Visit Latoya's website at LifeandaBudget.com.

- Liz from Friday Night Shenanigans. Visit Liz's website at FridayNightShenanigans.com.
- Ryan from Crazy Enough to Try. Visit Ryan's website at CrazyEnoughToTry.com.
- Jason from My Financial Answers. Visit Jason's website at MyFinancialAnswers.com.

ABOUT THE AUTHOR

Melanie Lockert is the personality behind the award-winning blog, Dear Debt, where she chronicled her journey out of $81,000 in student loan debt. Through her blog, she inspires readers to break up with debt by writing their very own breakup letter to debt.

In 2015, Melanie (and her journey out of debt) was named one of the top five most inspiring personal finance stories of the year by *Yahoo! Finance*. She currently works as a freelance writer and event planner. Melanie and her work have appeared in *Business Insider, The Huffington Post, Yahoo! Finance, INC,* and more.

Originally from the Los Angeles area, Melanie moved to New York City to attend New York University. She holds a Bachelor of Arts in Theater and a Master of Arts in Performance Studies. After stints in New York City and Portland, Oregon, she returned to Los Angeles, where she currently resides.

INDEX

CPSIA information can be obtained
at www.ICGtesting.com
Printed in the USA
LVOW04s1738111116
512626LV00008B/800/P